beaded bracelets

25 Dazzling Handcrafted Projects

CLAUDINE MCCORMACK JALAJAS

Running Press
PHILADELPHIA · LONDON

ISBN 978-0-7624-5316-0
Library of Congress Control Number: 2014939505

E-book ISBN 978-0-7624-5526-3

9 8 7 6 5 4 3 2 1
Digit on the right indicates the number of this printing
All illustrations by the author
Cover and interior design by Susan Van Horn
Technical editing by Susan Huxley
Edited by Sophia Muthuraj
Typography: Reverie, Mots Pro, Mr. Eaves, and Neutra

Running Press Book Publishers
2300 Chestnut Street
Philadelphia, PA 19103-4371

Visit us on the web!
www.runningpress.com

DEDICATION

For maman, who made me read every night before bed
and taught me that creating it yourself was better than buying it.

contents

introduction

I WALKED INTO A CRAFT STORE ONE DAY and noticed a jewelry demonstration with Swarovski AG Elements Crystals right by the doorway. It was impossible to miss the sparkle on the crystals, and I decided then and there that I needed to add jewelry making to my already long list of hobbies. I bought some wire and crimping beads and made a few pieces but decided I needed more inspiration. I went to my local library and looked through various bead magazines and came across patterns for woven bracelets, earrings, and necklaces. Having done counted cross-stitch for years my interest was piqued—I love detail and a challenge. I bought needles, thread, seed beads, and crystals. I. Was. Hooked.

I'm a busy working mom of three and, like most of us, I get stressed out with the many demands placed on me every day. I had tried meditation and yoga, but instead of relaxing I found myself wondering how much time had passed, spotting the guy who had fallen asleep, and noticing that the person next to me was breathing really loudly—annoying! Now bead weaving, on the other hand, provided me with the relaxation I craved. The attention to detail, repetitiveness, and focus provided me with the outlet I needed to relax AND be creative.

So after I would put my kids to bed at night I would take out the thread, needles, beads, and patterns and begin weaving. Soon I was getting up early in the morning to weave before the kids left for school and carrying my projects in my pocketbook just in case I had time to weave a few beads during the day. I loved the variety of seed bead colors and finishes and the softness of them.

How could glass beads feel like fabric or leather once woven together?

A large part of the fun for me is combining the different colors of beads. I like to put matte beads with shiny for contrast. And, combining beads with Swarovski crystals felt completely decadent because they're so precious—pricey, only available through authorized outlets, and the absolute pinnacle of quality. Do I wear a cuff bracelet covered in Swarovski crystals to the local store? Yes, I do. When I walk into a room people ask to look at my bracelet more closely and exclaim, "WHERE did you get this?" When I say that I made it they almost always say, "Where do you get the patience?" I usually just smile and thank them because let's face it, it only looks difficult. But between you, me, and the lamppost, it's not that hard. The truth is—all it takes is attention to detail and a little time.

Once you make a few pieces, you'll discover the advantage of custom jewelry. I hate to be uncomfortable. A metal or traditional cuff bracelet digs into my wrist when I put my arms down to type on the computer. I have small wrists too, so making my own bracelet allows me to make the bracelet fit perfectly for me.

Now I teach classes on bead weaving, and when I tell the participants that this will relax them, they always raise their eyebrows and snort. But after about 20 minutes they admit, "Hey, this is relaxing!" And the reason? Because every time you make a piece, you are focused directly on what is in front of you. It's not free-form work; you must pay attention to what you're doing, and meanwhile you will forget everything else from the day. It's part art and part therapy. It's a wonderful hobby with fantastic wearable rewards!

tools & materials

WEAVING JEWELRY REQUIRES few tools (which is great!), making it a very portable craft—I've worked on jewelry on trains, on planes, and every night while watching TV in bed. Do I sometimes hear beads hit the floor when I make the bed in the morning? Yes—but don't tell anyone.

The key tools you'll need are thread, needles, beads, bead glue, and a great pair of scissors.

NEEDLES

There are a lot of different beading needles out there, and at first glance they might not look much different than sewing needles. It's subtle but the needles for beading do not have a rounded eye (unless collapsible). The reason is that the needle has to go through a seed bead, so you need the eye to stay as narrow as the needle itself. If you use a sewing or a beading needle that's not the right size and force the needle through (true confession: I've done it), the bead will burst and then what you've got are teeny pieces of glass all over you. Let's say your needle does get stuck on a bead and you can't get the needle out from either side. In order to attempt to save the bead, I often will take a pair of pliers to grab the needle with one hand and hold the bead with my other hand and pull. This works 90 percent of the time without breaking the bead. If this doesn't work, a last resort is to use the same pliers to crush the stuck bead. Just do it over a trash can to save the bare feet in your home. So before doing anything, you should make sure the needle works for the size of bead you're using. Needles are generally sized by fine, medium, and large or by numbers like 10, 11, 12, 13; the larger the number the narrower the needle. They come in the following materials: nickel-plated carbon steel, carbon steel, steel, and stainless steel, which allows all not to rust and for some to flex while others stay very stiff.

There are also different lengths of needles. It took a while for me to find my groove with needles. It is part personal preference and part what you're working on. I tried a variety and finally settled on short sharps. The BeadSmith Short Beading Needles seem to fit most of the projects in this book quite well. Only two projects use size 15/0 beads. There are bendable needles that work well with weaving and are easy to thread, as they have a large eye that collapses as it goes through the bead. I have used the collapsible beading needles made by Beadalon, which are very easy to thread. I have also tried the Beadalon big eye needles, which are actually split down the entire center of the needle. The collapsible eyes are delicate and break easily and are not cheap, so I switched to the more indestructible BeadSmith 10 Shorts. Usually they come twenty to a pack (and I have a habit of losing them for some reason). Most needles are pretty inexpensive, so it doesn't hurt to throw a new pack in with your bead order to see what you think.

By the way, if you drop one they're REALLY hard to find, and if you don't want someone's bare foot to find it later, you should probably get down and look. I've used a large magnet from the fridge and waved it over the area where I assumed the needle was and it worked like a charm! But I would love to see them make beading needles out of metals in different bright colors—when they finally do that I want the credit.

THREAD

There are a lot of threads to choose from. Some people use thread that needs to be conditioned (coated to smooth and strengthen) before use. I have to be honest—I'm kind of lazy. So that is an extra step that I don't feel like taking.

My favorite threads are Beadalon® Wildfire and BeadSmith® Fireline. They're bonded threads that are strong and come in a few different thicknesses and pound test (strength). They're braided and already coated so there's no conditioning needed. Fireline doesn't stretch or tangle, threads nicely, and resists abrasion from beads with sharp or rough edges. If you are using crystals or bugle beads, I would suggest that you stick with one of these threads. Swarovski crystals often have sharp insides (remember—crystals are glass), and bugle beads are mainly metal and have sharp ends. Also, once you knot Fireline it's nearly impossible to undo. (See the chart in the back of the book for thread sizes and strength.)

Nymo thread is the most well-known thread. The nice thing about Nymo is that it's much less expensive than Wildfire or Fireline, and it comes in a wealth of colors, which means you can match the thread with your bead colors. You'll need to coat (most) Nymo with beeswax or some other thread conditioner if you want the thread (and bracelet) to last. There are some new Nymo threads that are waxed now and do not need to be conditioned before using. Nymo is sized a little differently. A bobbin of O is size fine, OO is size extra-fine, B is medium, and D is thicker. (See page 142 for reference).

CUTTING TOOLS

I like having a small pair of awesome scissors. Clean, nick-free edges means the end of snipped thread is a LOT easier to get through the eye of a beading needle. A nice pointy tip on the scissors means you can get in close so that no one sees your thread ends once you've finished your project. Get yourself a good pair of small scissors and hide them from the kids. You'd be surprised how quickly the blades will dull if the scissors are used to cut snowflakes out of construction paper.

Now, one little extravagant thing that I really love for finishing my projects is a threadburner. Scissors cannot get as close to the ends in your work as a burner can, so for finishing items it's great. The Fireline is a bonded material, so when you cut it with the burner it melts and you get a little bump on the end of the thread, making it lousy for threading on a beading needle. So that's why I call it extravagant. It's an expensive tool for a singular purpose. A word of caution—the tip of the burner is very delicate and easy to break. Put that cap back on when you're not using it. The tip can be replaced if you do break it, however.

You'll need a pair of solid wire cutters if you plan to make Freya (see page 105). The project is made with memory wire, which is extremely tough. Bypass this tool when shopping until you have a project that needs it.

BEADS & CRYSTALS

How Beads Are Sized

Seed beads come in sizes such as 15/0, 11/0, 8/0: the larger the number, the smaller the bead. Wait—what? That doesn't make sense, right? Well, seed beads are measured by how many can fit in an inch. (Another theory is that the bead size refers to the size of rod needed to make it.) So if fifteen beads in a row can fit into an inch, it's a 15/0 bead. If they're 8s then it means the bead is larger since only eight can fit in an inch. You'll always see "/0"; this isn't a number. It's the symbol for a unit of measurement called an aught.

How Crystals Are Sized

Crystals are sized in a more logical way. The bigger the number, the bigger the crystal. A 6mm crystal is larger than a 4mm crystal.

Special Types of Beads

Most seed beads that we're used to are round, but there are other types of seed beads, such as delica, cube, hex, triangle, magatama, Superduo, rulla, Rizo, and many more. There are new seed beads constantly being developed and introduced. This book contains patterns using some of these new beads, too!

NOTE: The projects in this book don't require a bead spinner, so cross that off your list.

BEAD GLUE

Bead glue is used to secure knots in these projects and also to add crystals to the ends of memory wire. GS Hypo cement is a medium strength glue that works well and is easily found in most bead shops or craft stores. It is not brittle and will not damage the thread, beads, or crystals. It dries clear and sets in 10-15 minutes.

where to buy, brands, and considerations

THERE ARE A FEW BEAD SHOPS out there, but I mainly order online as there are few that are close to my home. I also really like to go to bead shows, and you can find out about them coming to your area if you get on their mailing lists. A couple of the big shows are Tucson Bead Show, The Whole Bead Show, Innovative Bead Show, Intergalactic Bead and Jewelry Show, and Bead Fest.

If you don't mind waiting a few days for your order, online vendors are great. Most offer free shipping if you spend a certain amount, and you can't beat the variety of colors available. It's sometimes difficult to imagine how certain colors will work together, but I've called some vendors' support people and they've literally told me what colors go with what.

Another reason I use online distributors is that I can get Swarovski or Czech fire-polished crystals at a fraction of the price charged by a physical store, and I can be certain they're Swarovski. When you're out shopping, make sure you see the official licensing logo. I bought crystals once thinking they were Swarovski. They did not shine like real Swarovski and they were all cut differently. I wound up using them for ponytail holders for my daughter instead. I also like being able to buy exactly what I need. If I need thirty-three crystals, I can buy thirty-three online. I don't have to buy two packages of twenty-four (for example) and then have a small handful of leftover crystals.

For seed beads Toho Co., Ltd. is a reliable and cost-effective brand. Miyuki Co., Ltd. beads are superior and beautiful (but a little more expensive).

Whenever I saw an outrageous deal growing up, my mother would calmly reply, "I can't afford to buy cheap shoes, Claudine." I couldn't understand what she meant—we weren't buying shoes, and isn't spending less money a better way to afford things? My advice is the same as my mom's when it comes to buying beads—don't buy junk. You're creating these lovely pieces that take up your valuable personal time. Don't waste it with junky plastic seed beads and knockoff crystals. The seed beads won't be uniform or the right size, the color will rub off, and the shine will not be the same at all. One time, I was very pleased with my new blue woven bracelet and was later horrified when I noticed that there was blue all over my wrist from the cheap seed beads. The knockoff crystals look shiny under the lights in the store, but they will not sparkle like real Swarovski and will not be uniform in shape or size. What you choose to work with is often a matter of personal preference. Mind you, certain types, such as delicas, fit nicely when close together and have more consistency overall and in hole sizes, which really matters in weaving so your work lines up just right. Surface texture and iridescent quality or color depth can also affect the way the bead behaves and looks in the finished bracelet.

special note about instructions

THE MATERIALS LISTS SPECIFY THE EXACT NUMBER of larger or more expensive beads you need for each project. But seed beads are listed by the number of grams that you need because that's how they're sold. Depending on the distributor, you can get them in tubes or little bags. (You can also buy them—and most other beads—on loops of thread, called hanks.) In many instances I've included specific product names, specific colors, and the distributor's name to ensure you get the same results. The Resources section (see page 143) lists the websites and phone numbers so that you can order supplies. But this doesn't mean you have to use the same items that I did. Substitute at will, but try to stick to the size and type recommended. (For example, some types of thread, as mentioned earlier, are better choices for some beads, and certain beads are best suited to particular weaves.)

The finished size of each bracelet is listed. These measurements are approximate because the tension you use to weave will affect the outcome.

Weaving is rarely done on doubled thread, and all the projects in this book are done on one strand.

The illustrations in this book are color-coded so that it's easier for you to follow the sequence of actions. Blue beads are the ones that you're working on in the step. Light beads are the ones you've already worked with and are only shown for reference. If you have to pass through a previously threaded bead, it's red. These same colors are used when you embellish a strip of finished weaving, but that strip underneath is now light grey.

The quantity of beads to use is in spelled-out form so that it's not confused with the bead size number, which is in numerical form. Otherwise you might see "Thread 4 4mm pearls," and that gets confusing. Instead you'll see, "Thread four 4mm pearls."

Some of the bracelets have beads that vary only by size, or only by color. Whenever there's a chance these beads could be confused, in the Materials List I assign a letter to each one: A, B, and so on.

Finally, a piece of advice: keep your tension consistent. I have a tendency to keep a loose tension, and a friend of mine (who graciously helped me with many of the samples in this book!) uses a tighter tension. Our bracelets look the same but sometimes feel different, as mine are more loose and hers are firmer. It really just depends on your style—most important is that it is consistent.

the bracelets

springtime...25

flora...29

hide & seek...33

penelope...37

annabelle...43

champagne
bubbles...47

melissa's
honeybees...53

bridging the
gap...57

sea glass...63

tango...67

buckle up...71

hop scotch &
hinkesten...75

gatsby...81

stardust...85

crossword
puzzle...89

sea gold...95

he loves me, he loves me not...99

freya...105

aegis of athena...109

polaris...113

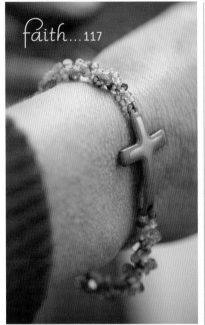

faith...117

brick by brick...121

serpentine...127

fleur de lis...131

eva...135

springtime

IF YOU KNEW ME, you would know that I love spring (and whine a lot about winter). Around December (I try to wait until after Christmas) I start to do a spring countdown on Twitter and Facebook. I've done this now for so many years that people will often tweet on particularly lousy winter days, "Hey, how many days are left?" Once I see the crocuses popping up in my yard, I know that no matter what the weather is at that moment—spring is coming soon.

This bracelet reminds me of small spring flowers such as bluebells, crocuses, and lilies of the valley. I covered the entire base of a very simple strip of right angle weave (RAW) technique with these adorable little flowers. This bracelet works up SO quickly you will love it. There are a slew of colors available with these flowers too, so go nuts.

Bracelet will be approximately ¼" wide and 7 ¼" long (25 sections), including the clasp.

MATERIALS LIST:

.006 Fireline thread

11/0 round seed beads, sunset orange TR (Bello Modo, 11-536 MAT): 8 grams

8/0 round seed beads, matte burgundy brown (Fusion Beads, SB1273): 8 grams

4mm x 6mm baby bell flower beads, dual coat peach/pear (Bello Modo, 123-46-48017): 35

Medium (13.5mm x 7mm) silver-plated lobster clasp (Artbeads, CLASP11-SP)

Bead glue

STEPS

1. Cut the thread 2 feet long and thread a needle, leaving a 6" tail.

2. Thread eight 11/0 beads. Go back through the first six beads you threaded in the same direction to form a circle.

3. Add six 8/0 seed beads. Go through the last two beads in the previous step.

4. Continue through the first four beads you added in this step.

5. Continue adding six beads at a time and going through the last two from the previous step for a total of twenty-five sections. You will either come from the top (step 5 illustration) or below (step 4 illustration).

Edge

6. After you have completed the twenty-five sections, fill the gaps between sections using the 11/0 seed beads. Go through the beadwork to the first gap, then add one seed bead. Go into the next two beads, add one seed bead, and go through the next two beads. Continue around the entire strand.

Flower Embellishment

7. From wherever you end up, go through the thread path so that you begin five sections from the end of your bracelet. Exit between two 8/O beads. Add one flower bead and one 11/O seed bead. Go around the seed bead and back through the flower and the next bead in the base.

8. Add flowers around the sections, following an S pattern, for fifteen sections.

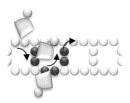

Clasp

9. On one end of the bracelet, add ten of the 11/O seed beads and go back into the beadwork, creating a loop for the lobster clasp. Go through the beads once or twice more to reinforce the loop. Finish with a half-hitch knot (see page 141), apply bead glue, and cut the thread once dry.

10. On the other end of the bracelet use the tail from step 1, add two seed beads, the lobster clasp end, and two seed beads. Go through the work a few times to reinforce the join. Finish with a half-hitch knot (see page 141), apply bead glue, and cut the thread once dry.

flora

FLORA IS THE GODDESS OF PLANTS, FLOWERS, AND FERTILITY in Roman mythology. I wanted this bracelet to resemble a strand of flowers and their leaves.

This bracelet uses the triangle technique.

Bracelet will be approximately ¾" wide and 6 ½" long (6 wagon wheels), not including the clasp.

MATERIALS LIST:

.006 Fireline thread

8/0 round seed beads, silver-lined matte red aurora borealis (AB) (Fusion Beads, SB0897): 10 grams

4 x 7mm Miyuki magatama beads, transparent green (Artbeads, LMA-179): 8 grams

4mm fire-polished (FP) round crystals (Artbeads, FPS-CRY4): 36

6mm Swarovski bicone crystals, fire opal (Artbeads, 5328-FIRE6): 6

14.5mm x 10.5mm gold-plated 2-strand snap clasp (Artbeads, CLASP19-GP)

Bead glue

STEPS

1. Cut the thread 1 yard long and thread a needle, leaving a 6" tail.

2. Thread three 8/0 seed beads, two magatama beads, three seed beads, and two magatamas. Go back through the first three seed beads and two magatamas, go through the next three seed beads, and exit before the remaining magatamas.

3. Add six 8/0 seed beads and go through the last three seed beads of the previous step and first three beads you added in this step. This is your first triangle. It may not look like one because the tension is loose at first, but as you add sections the triangles will become more obvious.

4. Thread six seed beads and go back through the last three beads you exited in the previous step and first

three seed beads you just added. Repeat this step until there are five triangles.

5. Create the last triangle by joining the first and fifth triangles together. Here is the process: Go up three seed beads on one side, add three seed beads, and go down through three seed beads on the adjacent triangle. This completes the wagon wheel.

6. Follow the thread path, as shown in the illustration, until you are at the top of the wagon wheel. Add two magatamas, three seed beads, two magatamas, and go through the three seed beads already in the wagon wheel marked red. Continue through the next two magatamas and three seed beads.

7. Follow steps 3 through 6 to add more wagon wheel units until you have reached the desired length (not including the length for the clasp).

Embellishment

8. Follow the thread path of the beads and get to the center of the nearest wagon wheel. Thread one FP crystal, cross the gap of the triangle, and go in between two seed beads on the opposite side. Since there are three beads it is impossible to go exactly in the middle, but it doesn't matter. It will look great. Continue filling each gap with FP crystals.

9. After adding the last FP crystal to the wagon wheel, thread a bicone crystal and pass through the opposite FP crystal on the other side of the flower.

10. Follow the thread path so that you end up at the next wagon wheel. Continue adding FPs and crystals until all of the wagon wheels are embellished.

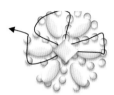

Clasp

11. Go through the beadwork to the clasp position. Add two seed beads, one clasp end, and two seed beads. Go back into the three seed beads at the end of the beadwork. Attach the other ring of the clasp in the same way. Go through the work you just did a few times to reinforce the join. Follow the thread path to the other end of the bracelet and attach the other part of the clasp in the same way. Finish with a half-hitch knot (see page 141), apply bead glue, and cut the thread once dry.

hide & seek

THIS IS A MULTISTRAND BRACELET done in tubular herringbone. This is a stitch that is fun to work with, and while it looks like it will take a while to create a rope this long, it does not.

The clasp is hidden behind the coral and crystal focal point of the piece. The clasp cover is done in two-drop peyote with 11/0 Toho seed beads and 3mm Czech fire-polished crystals.

Bracelet will be approximately ½" wide and 7 ½" long, wrapped.

MATERIALS LIST:

.006 Fireline thread

11/0 Toho round seed beads, transparent frosted green emerald (Artbeads, TBRD11-939F) color A: 8 grams

11/0 Toho round seed beads, aqua-lined jonquil (Artbeads, TBRD11-953) color B: 8 grams

3mm fire-polished (FP) crystals, hematite (Artbeads, FPS-HEM3): 15–20

14mm x 10mm two-strand magnetic tube clasp

Bead glue

STEPS

1. Cut the thread 1 yard long and thread a needle, leaving a 6" tail. Herringbone, as explained in the following steps, starts with a ladder stitch base. Create the ladder by piggy backing stacks of beads to form a solid base. Once you create the ladder base, you will form the rest of the bracelet with tubular herringbone.

2. Thread four color A 11/0 seed beads. Go through all four beads again forming two columns that are two beads high.

3. Add two more A seed beads and go through the previous two seed beads. Repeat one more time for a final count of four columns of two beads.

4. Fold the strip in half and join them together by going through the first two seed beads and last two seed beads you added.

5. Add four A seed beads and go down through the seed beads marked light blue. Come up through the seed beads marked red.

6. Flip your work. Add four A seed beads, going down two, and then back up through the other side.

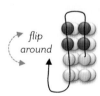

flip around

7. Add four A seed beads, go down two, and back up. The two sides will seem to be separate, but as you add sections you will be cinching the front and back together.

   Note: For purposes of these instructions the front will be red and the back will be blue. You will continually flip from front to back.

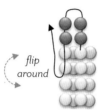

flip around

8. Continue adding rows until the length measures 14 ½" for a double-wrapped 7 ¼" bracelet (or whatever feels comfortable).

Clasp

9. Thread two B seed beads. Go through the magnetic clasp end and add two seed beads. Go through the beadwork on the opposite corner. Repeat on the other side of the bracelet with the tail you left in step 1. Finish with a half-hitch knot (see page 141), apply bead glue, and cut the thread once dry.

Clasp Cover

The clasp cover slides over the clasp to hide it but also holds the two straps of the bracelet together while wearing it. It is made with even-count two-drop peyote stitch (explained in the following steps) combining seed beads and FP crystals.

10. String one FP crystal and two B seed beads seven times.

The next row will build on the first by going in the opposite direction. Since the FP crystals are wider than the seed beads, you will have two seed bead rows for every one crystal row.

11. Add two B seed beads and go through the crystal from the previous row. Continue down the strip the same way.

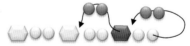

12. Turn by adding two B seed beads and going down through the seed beads in the previous row. Continue down the strip.

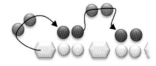

13. Make the turn with one FP crystal passing through the two seed beads from the previous row. Continue down the row until you get to the end.

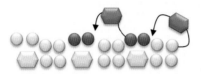

14. Add two B seed beads and make your turn. Continue down the row adding seed beads and passing through crystals.

15. Repeat the pattern until you have fourteen rows of beads, counting rows as shown below.

16. Bring the two sides together to form a tube, making sure that when they are joined (later in this step) the pattern is still the same: crystal and two rows of seeds. If it is not going to match, add a row of whatever is missing. To make the tube, exit the last two seed beads and cross to the opposite side and sew through the crystal marked in blue below, cross over to the opposite side of the tube and sew through that crystal. Follow the red beads in the illustration. Once across, go back through to the other side to make a strong connection.

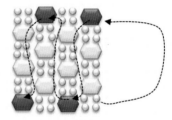

Slide the tube over the bracelet strand and weave the strand through the tube one more time. When worn, close the clasp and slide the tube over the clasp.

penelope

PENELOPE WAS THE BEAUTIFUL AND FAITHFUL WIFE of Odysseus, the king of Ithaca, in Homer's *The Odyssey*. While Odysseus was on his journey, many wanted to court her, but she kept them at bay by telling them she would have to finish her weaving first. What no one knew, though, was that she was undoing the piece she was working on to keep the suitors waiting. Her plan worked. She wasn't done before Odysseus returned and reunited with her many years later.

This bracelet won't take as long as it took Penelope, but just be prepared that it will take a little longer than some of the other projects in this book. I love cube beads. They are remarkably comfortable to wear, and because of their size they work up really fast. When it's done, the bracelet has a gorgeous look to it and wears great. It feels a lot like lace.

Bracelet will be approximately 1 ½" wide and 6 ¾" long (20 rows), before clasp. Each row is five sections wide. Each section is approximately ¼" wide and long.

MATERIALS LIST:

.006 Fireline thread

11/0 Toho round seed beads, purple-lined light topaz (Artbeads, TBRD11-926): 8 grams

3mm cube beads, olive-lined golden (Beadin' Path, CB3-F463R): 30 grams

30mm x 10mm five-strand tube slide clasp

STEPS

1. Cut the thread 1 yard long and thread a needle, leaving a 6" tail.

2. You will be adding thread on this bracelet, as it takes quite a bit to complete this bracelet. (See page 140 to learn the process.) Thread two seed beads. Go through the beads just threaded, in the same direction, and push the two beads so that they are side by side.

3. Add a cube bead and go through the previous two seed beads and once more through the cube. This will fasten the cube to the two seed beads.

4. Add two seed beads and go through the cube and two seed beads you just added.

5. Add two seed beads and go through the two seed beads added in step 4.

6. Add two seed beads and go through the remaining two seed beads.

7. Add two seed beads and go back through the two beads you just exited and then again through the two you just added.

8. Repeat steps 3 through 7 until you have five cubes across ending with only one set of seed beads on the end of the strip. This is the width of your bracelet. If you want it narrower or wider, you can add/remove cubes. Each cube with seed beads is ¼" wide and long.

ROW 2

9. Follow the thread path through the beads to get to the bottom of the last (marked red) cube's seed beads and add two seed beads.

10. Go back through the first two beads you started on and the two new beads you just added.

11. Add a cube and go back through the beads you just added. Go through the cube again.

12. Add two seed beads and go through the cube and the beads you just added. It's important that with every addition of beads you cross through the cube. It will prevent the cubes from flipping up later when the bracelet is finished!

13. Add two seed beads and go through the seed beads on the top of the current cube. Add two seed beads and go around all the seed beads until you get through the beads you just added).

14. Add two seed beads to the ones you just added. Go through the two you added in the previous step and the two you just added.

15. Add a cube to the side of the set you just added. Go through the seed beads you just exited and the cube you just added.

16. Add two seed beads. Go through the cube and the seed beads you just added.

17. Add two seed beads. Go through the beads shown in red and add two seed beads. Go through the two seed beads above (shown in green), back through the beads you just added, and down through the side beads (shown in red).

18. Repeat steps 14 through 17 to finish the row. Continue adding rows until the bracelet is the desired length, not including the clasp.

Clasp

With a multistrand clasp, it's not always possible to line up the cubes and seed beads exactly. Just do the best you can as far as being balanced and centered. Since this bracelet is the same on both sides, there is no front or back to contend with. Go through the beads to get to the end of your bracelet and line up to the clasp position.

19. Add two seed beads, go through the ring on the end of the clasp, add two seed beads, and go into the beadwork. Go through the work a few times to reinforce the join. Repeat with the remaining rings.

20. Use the tail on the opposite end of the bracelet and add the other part of the clasp end in the same way.

annabelle

MY DAUGHTER AND I have been in the garden digging and planting together since I had her in the Baby Bjorn®. She's eight years old now and even though our gardens are overflowing with flowers, year after year she begs to go to the nursery and get even MORE flowers. Every spring I smile when I hear her yell from outside, "MOM! A tulip bloomed! A tulip bloomed!" She does not tire of their beauty. And since she has known how to use a pair of scissors, she has cut flowers (including dandelions) and thrust them toward me with pride, "Look what I brought you." Because of her, we have fresh-cut flowers from our garden in the house all spring and summer.

The idea for this bracelet came to me when I was looking at my adorable flower beads. I thought it would be great to make the beads look like they were growing on a garden trellis. When I saw how lovely the flowers looked together, I couldn't help but think of my daughter and her love of flowers. Her name is Annabelle. This bracelet uses the right angle weave (RAW) technique.

Bracelet will be approximately ½" wide and 7 ½" long (33 square units), including the clasp. Each section is ¼" long. This bracelet is designed so that the clasp is under the bracelet and flowers.

MATERIALS LIST:

.006 Fireline thread

3mm bugle beads, matte transparent cobalt aurora borealis (AB) (Fusion Beads, SB0703): 10 grams

11/0 Toho round seed beads, wisteria-lined crystal (Artbeads, TBRD11-935): 8 grams

5mm x 6mm baby bell Czech glass flowers (Fusion Beads, GL8867): 12

14mm x 10mm two-strand tube slide clasp

Bead glue

STEPS

1. Cut the thread 1 yard long and thread a needle, leaving a 6" tail.

2. Thread four bugle beads. Go through the bugles in the same direction and then back through the first to form a square.

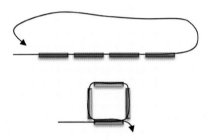

3. Thread three bugles and go back through the bead you exited. This is one unit.

4. Go through the first bugle and add three bugles. Go up through the side bugle of the top square.

5. Add two bugles and go through the top bugle of the square immediately below. Continue through the bugles in this bottom square as shown in the illustration.

6. Continue adding square units for the length of the bracelet (do not deduct the clasp length because it is under the bracelet and flowers). Each section is approximately ¼" long.

Embellishment

First, embellish the trellis with seed beads simulating leaves and vines. Each row will have alternating clusters of seed beads. Then add the glass flower beads to each end of the bracelet.

ROW 1

7. Starting at the corner of the bracelet, add one seed bead in the gap between the two bugle beads. Follow the thread path to the next gap and add three seed beads. Continue along the upper outer edge, alternating between adding one seed bead and then three seed beads to the opposite corner.

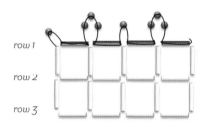

ROW 2

8. If there are three seed beads in row 1, add one seed bead, go through the center bead of the three beads in row 1, add one bead, and go back into the next row 2 gap. This will join row 1 and row 2 with a small cluster of seeds. When there is one bead in row 1, add three seed beads in the row 2 gap (which you will cluster to row 3), and continue to the next row 2 gap.

9. Repeat step 8 to the end of the bracelet.

ROW 3

10. Starting from the corner of the bracelet, add one seed bead in the gap between the two bugles. Follow the thread path to the next gap, and if row 2 was clustered between rows 1 and 2, add one seed bead. If row 2 had three unclustered seed beads, add one bead, go through the center bead in the row 2 cluster, and add another seed bead. Go into the next bugle. Continue along the bottom outer edge.

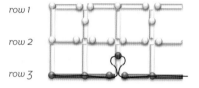

Flower Embellishment

11. Starting with the second column of squares from the end of the bracelet, add one baby bell flower and one seed bead. Go back through the flower, into the gap you just exited, and through to the next gap. In this way, add six flowers to the end of the bracelet, go through the beadwork to the opposite end, and add six flowers.

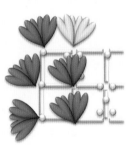

Clasp

12. Flip the bracelet over. Go through the beadwork to the gap between the first and second columns of bugles. Add two seed beads, go through the clasp end, add two seed beads, and go into the beadwork. Go through the work a few times to reinforce the join. Repeat with the other ring.

13. Move through the beadwork or use the tail on the other ring of the clasp end and attach in the same way. Finish with a half-hitch knot (see page 141), apply bead glue, and trim the thread once dry.

14. Add the other part of the clasp to the gap between the first and second row. Knot the thread, glue, and trim.

champagne bubbles

WHEN I LOOK AT THIS BRACELET I think of a good friend of mine. She is incredibly honest and does not fawn unless she means it. The first time she saw this bracelet she immediately liked it and asked me to make her one. When I said to her that I liked the bubbly texture of the bracelet, she said, "It's like champagne!" (She also happens to love champagne.) When I look at this bracelet I cannot separate the two.

This bracelet uses the right angle weave (RAW) technique.

Bracelet will be approximately ½" wide and 6 ¾" long (22 sections), including 1" clasp.

MATERIALS LIST:

.006 Fireline thread

4mm pearls: 112

3mm Czech fire-polished (FP) crystals, color A: 33

3mm Czech FP crystals, color B: 32

15/0 Toho round seed beads, gold lustered transparent pink (Artbeads, TBRD15-421): 3 grams

14mm antique box clasp (Elegant Elements, Bello Modo)

Bead glue

STEPS

1. Cut the thread 1 yard long and thread a needle, leaving a 6" tail.

2. Thread four pearls. Go through all the beads in the same direction to form a circle. Continue once more through the first three pearls.

3. Thread three pearls. Go through the pearl you first exited and go through the next two pearls.

4. Repeat step 3 for twenty-two sections, or your desired length of bracelet (not including the clasp).

ROW 2

5. Follow the thread path and continue to top pearl. Add three pearls and go through the pearl you first exited and the first one added in this step.

6. Add two pearls and go through the second pearl in the row, the first pearl you exited, the new pearls, and the top pearl beside where you are working (shown in red).

7. Add two pearls. Go through the pearls shown in red. Repeat this step across the length of the bracelet.

Embellishment

8. From the last pearl in the bracelet, add a Czech FP crystal color A and cross over the gap in the pearls, going through the pearl shown in red. It will be across the pearl section on an angle. Continue down the bracelet, alternating between adding color A and color B crystals.

10. From the last pearl in the bracelet, continue to the bottom row by entering the pearl. Add a color B crystal to your thread (or whatever is opposite to the top row). Cross over the gap in the pearls and go through the pearl marked red. It will be across the pearl section on an angle like the top row. Continue down the bracelet, alternating between color A and color B crystals.

9. From the center pearl, exit and add a crystal in the color you ended with in the previous step. Go through the next pearl. Repeat, alternating colors, to the end of the bracelet.

11. Follow the thread path shown in the illustration. Add two 15/0 seed beads and step through the next pearl. Continue around the entire bracelet until you are back where you began.

Clasp

12. From a corner pearl, add two 15/0 seed beads; go around one of the clasp ends and back through the two seed beads you just added. Go through the pearls in a circle and back through the seed beads into the clasp end again to reinforce the join.

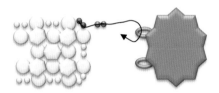

13. Use the tail on the opposite corner pearl. Repeat step 12. Add the clasp to the other side of the bracelet with the tail you left in the beginning, at step 2. Finish with a half-hitch knot (see page 141), apply bead glue, and cut the thread once dry.

melissa's honeybees

THIS BRACELET, ADORNED WITH LARGE FLOWERS, makes me think of the honeybees in summer that frighten my children but that my Labradors love to chase. It is named after Melissa, a nymph from Greek mythology who discovered honey and gave the bees their name. Melissa also happens to be a friend of mine that helped me tremendously with this book and to whom I will always be grateful.

The base of this bracelet uses the right angle weave (RAW) technique and can be done with small 3mm pearls, Druk beads, or any 3mm rounds. The seed beads can be either 8/0 or 11/0. Using 11/0 beads makes the bracelet slightly stiffer and takes a little longer to complete (and more materials). The 8/0 beads give you a more loose-fitting bracelet (similar to a chainmail bracelet). The following directions are for 11/0 beads.

Bracelet will be approximately 1 ½" wide and 6 ½" long (34 rows), not including the clasp.

MATERIALS LIST:

.006 Fireline thread

3mm Swarovski (5810) round pearls, petrol*: 250 – 300

11/0 Toho round seed beads, opaque shiny jet black: 8 grams

15mm x 6mm Czech dagger beads, wasabi: 36

4mm Czech fire-polished (FP) beads, crystal/copper: 18

30mm x 10mm five-strand tube slide clasp

Bead glue

* Pearls, Czech Druk beads, or any 3mm rounds will do.

STEPS

1. Cut the thread 1 yard long and thread a needle, leaving a 6" tail.

2. Thread one pearl, one seed bead, one pearl, and one seed bead. Go through the four beads again to form a diamond. Continue through the next three beads.

3. Thread one seed bead, one pearl, and one seed bead. Go through the pearl you exited at the beginning of this step and the next two (seed bead and pearl) you just added.

4. Repeat step 3 until you have ten pearls across.

ROWS

In the following steps you add rows so that the bracelet is the desired length, not including the clasp. You will need approximately thirty-four rows and a ¾" clasp for a 7 ¼" long bracelet.

5. Turn the beadwork sideways. Exit through the closest seed bead. Thread one pearl, one seed bead, and one pearl. Continue through the bead you first exited and the three beads just added. Go through the next seed bead. Add one pearl and one seed bead. Go through the pearl you added previously, the seed bead you just exited, and down through the next seed bead in the strip. Repeat across the strip.

6. Turn the beadwork to add another row in this step. Add one pearl, one seed, and one pearl. Go through the seed bead you exited and the beads just added. Go up through the next seed bead shown in red. Add one pearl and one seed bead. Go through the last bead you added previously. Repeat across the strip.

Flower Adornment

TIP: You can add the flower adornments however you like, but I prefer mine to be askew instead of in a neat row. I add the first one in the center and closer to one side of the bracelet. The other two are on the opposite sides. It's important to keep them clustered in the center if you want them to be on top when the bracelet is worn. Otherwise, they wind up on the sides. This doesn't look as fantastic.

7. Go through the beadwork to the center of the bracelet. Go through two pearls from the edge and come up through the third, add one 15mm x 6mm dagger bead to make the first petal, go down through the next pearl, add another dagger, and continue around in the same way until you have six petals.

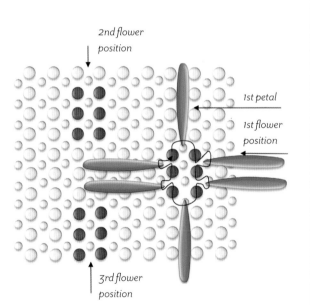

2nd flower position

1st petal

1st flower position

3rd flower position

8. Come up through the first dagger and add another dagger. Go through the next dagger and add another dagger. Continue around to the first petal, adding more daggers and slightly tugging on your thread to snug up the daggers.

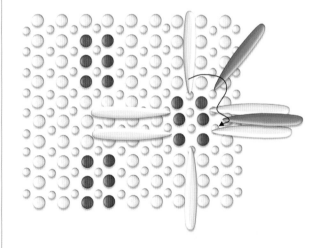

9. Go through the first dagger and add one Czech FP bead. Cross over to the opposite petal marked green (see illustration) and go through that dagger and the one beside it. Add two FP beads and cross over to the opposite flower dagger shown in red. Go through both red daggers, add two FP beads, and go through both purple daggers. Add one FP bead and cross over to the opposite dagger marked in orange. Go through all the daggers one more time, pulling the thread to tighten the daggers to each other.

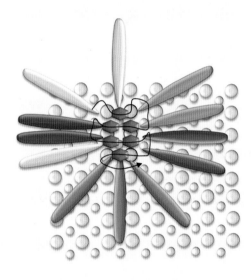

10. Add two more flower adornments to the bracelet in the same way.

Clasp

With a multistrand clasp, it's not always possible to line up the beads and seeds exactly. Just do the best you can as far as being balanced and centered. Get to the end of your bracelet and line up the clasp with your bracelet.

11. Go through the beadwork to one end of the bracelet. Add two seed beads, go through one ring of the clasp end, add two seed beads, and go into the beadwork at the end of the bracelet. Go through the work a few times to reinforce the join. Repeat this process to secure the other rings.

12. Use the tail on the oppposite end of the bracelet and add the other part of the clasp in the same way. Finish with a half-hitch knot (see page 141), add drop of bead glue to your knots, and trim the thread once dry.

bridging the gap

I PERSONALLY LIKE TO MAKE THIS BRACELET with a variety of colors. The stitching is not difficult and works up quickly. All the random colors give it a lot of texture and make it look more complicated than it really is. The best way to stay random is not to think about the pearls you're picking up. Dump them all in a cup and then pick them up haphazardly. Just reach in and go with it.

This set of instructions has two options. The green bracelet pictured has a narrower center with a smaller bridge. You'll need a few extra beads to do the pink bracelet because it has a larger gap in the center. Which you choose to make depends on how much you want to see the gap.

This bracelet uses the right angle weave (RAW) technique.

Pink bracelet will be approximately 1" wide and 6 ½" long (22 rows), not including the clasp. Green bracelet will be approximately ¾" wide and 6" long (22 rows), not including the clasp.

MATERIALS LIST:

.006 Fireline thread

11.4mm x 10.5mm gold-filled 2-strand filigree pearl clasp (Artbeads, GF-PC04): 1

Bead glue

PINK VERSION

4mm Swarovski (5810) round pearls, neon pink and rosaline: 160

11/0 Toho round seed beads, lined dark coral/crystal (Artbeads, TBRD11-185): 8 grams

3mm fire-polished (FP) beads, sapphire aurora borealis (AB) (Artbeads, FPS-SAPAB3): 1 pack (120 pieces)

GREEN VERSION

4mm glass pearls, emerald isle mix (Artbeads, PMX-EMR4): 2 packs (50 pieces)

11/0 Toho round seed beads, moss green-lined yellow (Artbeads, TBRD11-947): 8 grams

3mm fire-polished (FP) beads, emerald green AB (Artbeads, FPS-EMR3): 1 pack (120 pieces)

STEPS

1. Cut the thread 1 yard long and thread a needle leaving a 6" tail.

2. Thread four pearls. Go through all the beads in the same direction to form a circle. Continue once more through the first three pearls.

3. Thread three pearls and go through the pearl you first exited. Go through the next two pearls. This completes one section.

4. Repeat step 3 for 22 sections, or until the desired length is reached, allowing for the clasp.

Bridge

5. After adding the last ring of pearls, follow the thread-path and continue through to the third one you added. Add three pearls. Go through the pearl you first exited and the first two you just added.

ROW 2

6. Add three pearls and go through the pearl you first exited and the first two new ones.

7. For the larger gap (pink version), repeat step 6. For the narrower gap (green version), continue to step 8.

8. Add three pearls and go through the pearl you first exited and the first two pearls just added.

9. Repeat step 8, alternating coming from the top or bottom, until one section from the end of the bracelet.

Bridge End

10. Add three pearls and go through the pearl you first exited. Go through the three pearls you just added.

11. Add three pearls and go through the pearl you first exited. Continue through the first two pearls you just added.

12. Add one pearl and connect to the bottom pearl. Add another pearl and go through the pearl you first exited and the pearls just added to reinforce the join.

Crystal Embellishment

13. From the last pearl in the bracelet, add a seed bead, a 3mm FP bead, and a seed bead. Cross over the gap in the pearls and go through the pearl (shown in red). It will be across the top of the pearl section on an angle. Continue adding seed beads and FP beads down the bracelet, up the bridge, and back down the other side of the bracelet.

Interior Embellishment

14. Exit the bottom pearl shown in red and add eight seed beads. (You may need to add 10 to fit the larger gap.) Cross over to the top pearl shown in red, skipping a grouping of pearls for guidance in distance (shown in grey).

15. Cross to the other side, using the same distance of skipping one grouping of pearls as your guide.

16. Repeat steps 14 and 15, going all the way down the beadwork and then back across in the other direction to form an x pattern.

Clasp

17. Add two seed beads, one ring of the clasp end, and two seed beads. Go through the end of the bead-work and through the work you just did a few times to reinforce the join. Attach the other ring of the same clasp end in the same way. Follow the thread path to the other end of the bracelet and attach the other end of the clasp in the same way. Finish with a half-hitch knot (see page 141), add drop of bead glue to your knots, and trim the thread once dry.

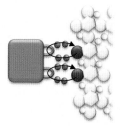

sea glass

EVERY YEAR MY KIDS GIVE ME FLOWERS (and most recently, trees!) for the garden for my Mother's Day gifts. A couple years ago I hinted that I would love an arbor over the front gate and so my husband and sons made a beautiful one! I thought it would be nice to create a bracelet that reminded me of the garden trellis with roses beside it, but when I laid this bracelet down on the counter, the first thing my son Max said was, "Oh, wow that looks like sea glass on the beach." So what do you see—flowers on a trellis or sea glass sparkling on the beach? Either way, I love the contrast between the matte bugle beads and the seed beads with the brilliant sparkle of the crystal flowers.

This bracelet uses the right angle weave (RAW) technique.

Bracelet will be approximately 1 ½" wide and 7" (33 bugle rows) long, not including the clasp.

MATERIALS LIST:

.006 Fireline thread

8/0 round seed beads, light blue-lined transparent matte dark blue (Fusion Beads, SB1020): 30 grams

12mm twisted bugle beads, matte transparent light kelly green aurora borealis (AB) (Fusion Beads, SB0765): 10 grams

14mm Preciosa Czech crystal flower, blue zircon (Fusion Beads, PC6662): 1

11/0 Toho round seed beads, emerald-lined amber (Artbeads, TBRD11-242): 8 grams

8mm Swarovski crystal flower margarita (Fusion Beads, EW0698): 8

6mm Swarovski crystal flower margarita (Fusion Beads, EW0661): 2

30mm x 10mm five-strand tube slide clasp

Bead glue

STEPS

1. Cut the thread 1 yard long and thread a needle, leaving a 6" tail.

2. Thread four 8/0 seed beads. Go through all the seed beads, in the same direction, and then go through the second one you added. Add one bugle.

3. Add four 8/0 seed beads and go through the seed beads again, ending after the third one you added. Add one bugle bead and go through the bottom bead (shown in red) on the opposite side.

4. Add three 8/0 seed beads and go through the bead you first exited and through the first two of the new beads you just added.

5. Add one bugle and two 8/0 seed beads. Go through the closest seed bead of the previous row, add one 8/0 seed bead, and go through the first seed bead you added.

6. Add three 8/0 seed beads, pass through the bead you first exited and the first two you added. Add a bugle. Continue adding rows until you have reached your desired bracelet length, not including the clasp.

ROW 2

7. From the outer side seed bead in the bottom row, add three 8/0 seed beads. Go through the bead you first exited and the first bead you added.

8. Add a bugle and four 8/0 seed beads. Pass through the first three again. Add a bugle and go through the two beads shown in red. Add two 8/0 seed beads and go through the two seed beads shown in red again.

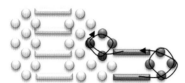

9. Exit the seed bead shown in red and add a bugle. Add two 8/0 seed beads, go through the top bead of the bottom row (shown in red), add one 8/0 seed bead, and go through the first seed bead you added. Add three more seed beads and go through the first two again in the same direction. Continue adding seed beads and bugles to the end of the strip.

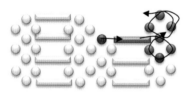

10. Follow the thread path to the center of the bracelet. Come up through a seed bead. Add the 14mm crystal flower and an 11/0 seed bead. Go around the seed bead and back through the flower. Add eight 8mm flowers down the center and one 6mm flower on either end of floral cluster. The flowers should be clustered together as they often are in nature.

Clasp

11. Follow the beadwork to the end of the bracelet. Add two 8/0 seed beads, go through the clasp ring on the end, add two seed beads, and go into the beadwork. Go through the work a few times to reinforce the join.

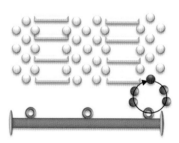

12. Use the tail from step 1 to add the other part of the clasp in the same way. Finish with a half-hitch knot (see page 141), apply bead glue, and cut the thread once dry.

tango

THE TANGO IS A DANCE WHERE THE TWO DANCERS must always be touching. This bracelet is made of two strips of herringbone joined together with Czech fire-polished crystals.

This bracelet uses the herringbone technique (also referred to as nde-bele). Using large cube beads means this bracelet whips up quickly, and the texture of the beads means it's incredibly comfortable to wear as well. Going out dancing tonight? You can whip this up, throw on an awesome dress, and be properly accessorized in your Tango bracelet.

Bracelet will be approximately 1 ½" wide and 7 ¼" long. Two additional rows to each end is ¼".

MATERIALS LIST:

.006 Fireline thread

3mm cube beads, silver-lined transparent cranberry aurora borealis (AB) (Fusion Beads, SB0171) color A: 10 grams

3mm cube beads, jet peacock iris (Beadin' Path, CB3-452) color B: 10 grams

11/0 round seed beads, dark grey luster (Beadin' Path, SDB11-178): 3 grams

4mm Czech fire-polished (FP) crystals, matte ruby (AB): 25

14mm x 10mm two-strand tube slide clasp

Bead glue

STEPS

1. Cut the thread 1 yard long and thread a needle, leaving a 6" tail.

    TIP: Ladder stitch is used to start a design done in herringbone. You create a band two beads wide because the herringbone stitch uses an even number of beads.

Ladder Stitch

2. To make a ladder, thread two color A cube beads. Go through both beads again in the same direction. The beads should be side by side, with both openings facing up and the closed edges beside each other.

3. Your thread should be coming straight up from your beadwork. Flip your work if it is not. Pick up (add) one color A and one color B and go down through the first cube you added in the previous step.

4. To turn, add two seed beads and go up through the last cube you added. (The turn seed beads will not be on every row.)

5. Add two color B cubes and go down through the cube in the previous row. Turn adding two seed beads and going up through second cube you added.

6. Add one color B cube and one color A cube; turn. Follow the pattern shown until you have reached the desired length allowing for clasp.

AA	
BA	
BB	
AB	
(Row 1) AA	

7. After you have stitched the final row, go through each of the beads across the final row, tightening them up to each other to create an identical ladder row to the ladder row in the beginning.

8. Make a second strip, but skip step 7. It's easier to add or remove length if you leave this strip unfinished.

Joining Strips

9. Use ends you started with and flip the strips so that the outside turn beads are on alternating rows. Add one cube (opposite color) to one strip by piggy backing to the cube next to it. Add another cube (opposite color) and piggy back to the cube you just added and then to the second strip. Flip the bracelet and join the other end the same way.

10. Follow the thread path up through the batch of interior double seeds (the turn beads, shown in red). Add one FP crystal and go through the opposite turn beads. Add one FP crystal and cross over to the other turn beads (shown in red).

11. Follow up through the next cube (shown in red). Repeat the last step and then go through the next cube on the other side. Continue like this to the end of the bracelet.

TIP: You may not have enough room, depending on the length of your bracelet, to end the inner embellishment evenly. End with one FP crystal or leave an extra space.

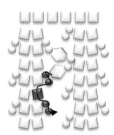

12. Join the bottom of the strips like you did in step 9.

Clasp

13. Add two seed beads and go through the first ring on the clasp end. Add two more seed beads and go back down through the cubes. Go to the next set of cubes and up through the ring in the clasp end. Follow the thread path a few times to secure the join. Use the tail on the other side of the bracelet. Add other side of clasp. Finish with a half-hitch knot (see page 141), apply bead glue, and cut the thread once dry.

buckle up

I LOVE THIS BRACELET mainly because of the buckle. I've made it a couple times using different buckles I've found in bead shops. It's not easy to find cool buckles, but once you do, make this bracelet! The beadwork is peyote. There is a little beaded strip in the center that keeps the buckle in position so it does not slide. It's just a fun and funky bracelet.

Bracelet will be approximately 1 ½" wide and 6 ½" long, not including the clasp.

MATERIALS LIST:

.008 Fireline thread

11/0 Toho round seed beads, gold-lustered violet (Artbeads, TBRD11-205): 1 gram

8/0 Toho hex beads, higher-metallic royal purple (Artbeads, TBHX8-461): 30 grams

56mm x 34mm buckle with center bar

20mm x 10mm three-strand tube slide clasp

Bead glue

STEPS

1. Cut 1 yard of thread and thread a needle. You will need a lot of thread for this bracelet, so you should use the longest piece you can handle (without getting yourself tied up) or add thread later (see Adding New Thread, page 000).

2. Take a seed bead that you are not using and thread it. Put your needle through it again to secure it. Do not knot it. You will remove this stop bead when you are ready to add the clasp.

3. Thread sixteen hex beads.

4. Add another hex to make your turn. The first turn can sometimes be tricky. You will want to maintain a consistent tension so that the beads form the correct pattern. The beads will line up as shown. Skip the second bead on the thread and put your needle through the third hex.

5. Continue down the row, adding a hex and skipping one bead.

6. Once you have reached the end, you will need to turn again. Go through the last bead in the row and add a hex. (If it is easier, flip your work so you are going from the same direction as before.) Go through the second hex in the row like you did on your first turn.

7. Continue adding rows until you have reached 6 ½" or your desired length, not including the clasp.

Buckle

TIP: To add the buckle, you will use the stitch-in-the-ditch technique. This is used when you want to add a layer on top of an existing layer worked in peyote stitch. You add a layer, add the buckle, and then close the layer. This way the buckle doesn't move on the bracelet—it's a fixed adornment. Placement of the buckle is the tricky part, as there is no way to be certain that you're perfectly in the center. Estimate and get as close as possible. Once the bracelet is on, you won't be able to tell if the buckle is perfectly centered, or not, anyway.

8. The buckle will require about ten to twelve rows of hexes on top of your current peyote-stitch base. Find the center of your bracelet and count back four rows.

9. Thread a needle. Enter the beadwork from the side of the bracelet.

   TIP: The center portion needs to be able to fit through the buckle, so make sure the beadwork isn't too wide or too small, and adjust your work accordingly. The width should come as close to the inner edges of the buckle as possible.

10. At the first gap, add one hex. Go down through the next hex. Come up and add another hex. Continue across as shown.

11. Turn your work and add another hex. Instead of going into the base, go into your newly added beads. Continue across in the same way.

12. Continue for about ten rows. Put the new strip of peyote through the buckle. Attach to the bracelet using the stitch-in-the-ditch technique again. Go through the beadwork alternating between the strip you just added and base of bracelet. Turn and alternate the beads so that you form a secure join. Tie off with a half-hitch knot (see page 141), add bead glue to the knot, and trim your thread once dry. It is slightly more difficult since you will need to work around the buckle.

13. Work your way to the end of the bracelet. Coming through the last hex in the row, add two seed beads and go under the next hex. Repeat on the other end of the bracelet. This will fill in the gaps.

Clasp

14. Remove the stop bead by gently pulling it away from the beadwork. Add two seed beads, go through the end clasp ring, add two more seed beads, and go into the beadwork. Go through the work a few times to reinforce the join.

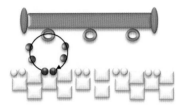

15. Move through the beadwork to add the next ring of the clasp in the same way. Repeat with the remaining ring. Finish with a half-hitch knot (see page 141), apply bead glue, and cut the thread once dry.

hopscotch & hinkesten

DID YOU KNOW THAT IN DENMARK they play hopscotch with a beautiful piece of purchased glass instead of a rock? The glass is often multicolored or has etchings on the top of it. When I learned about this, I was shocked. I'm not sure I would ever use mine for hopscotch! They're too pretty. I would make a bracelet out of mine instead.

NOTE: Each strip on the bracelet will have three of the Swarovski two-hole settings on it. The strips will only be joined on the ends of the bracelet, giving the illusion of being a multistrand yet wearing like a cuff.

Bracelet will be approximately 1 ¼" (4 squares) wide and 6 ¾" long, not including the clasp. Each row of square sections is ¼" long.

.006 Fireline thread

1.5mm Miyuki square-cut delica beads, metallic rainbow matte turquoise/light green: 8 grams

11/0 Toho round seed beads, mauve-lined frosted crystal: 8 grams

6.5mm Swarovski crystals in two-hole, gold-plated setting, light amethyst (17704 SS29 Xilion): 12

30mm x 10mm five-strand tube slide clasp

Bead glue

STEPS

1. Cut the thread 1 yard long and thread a needle, leaving a 6" tail.

2. String eight delica beads. Go back through the first four to create a square.

3. Add one seed bead and pass through two delicas.

4. Add another seed bead. Continue around the square, filling in each corner. Follow the thread path, exiting the beadwork the first seed you added and between delicas.

5. Add two delicas and go through the closest two delicas to attach. Continue through the two new delicas you just added.

6. Add six more delicas. Go through the two you added in the previous step.

7. Add one seed bead, pass through the next two delicas, add one seed bead, pass through the next two delicas, and add one seed bead. Pass through the last two delicas added in the previous step and add one seed bead. Pass through the delicas and seed beads you added until you are at the bottom right corner.

8. Repeat steps 5 through 7 until you have four squares in a row. This is the width of your bracelet.

9. Add two delicas to the side of the new square, to start the second connected row of squares. Repeat step 6 and 7.

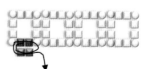

10. Add two delicas to the top of the new square (shown in red). Go back through the delicas you just added and add six more delicas. Go up through the two delicas on the side of the nearest square in row 1.

11. Add a seed bead. Continue through the next two delicas you added in the last step. Repeat adding seed beads in each corner and passing through the next two delicas until you are back at the first seed bead you added in this step. Repeat steps 9 – 11 two more times to create two more squares.

12. Add two delicas and go through the two delicas of the closest square to secure.

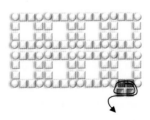

13. Add six more delicas. Continue around the square, adding seed beads in each corner. Continue adding square sections until the strip is four rows wide and seven long.

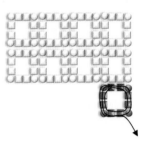

14. Add two delicas to the square section you just created. Go through a two-hole setting crystal, add two delicas, and go back through the crystal on the other side. Go through the two delicas you started with, then the crystal and the two newer delicas.

15. Repeat steps 12 – 14 until there are a total of of three crystal settings. After adding the third crystal, add eight square sections (steps 9 – 11).

16. Mirror the opposite end of the bracelet with two joined rows. Follow the thread path through the joined row to the starting position of the second row in the strip. Create additional strips, reversing the order of squares and crystals each time for a total of four rows.

   TIP: Each row will be like this illustration; five square sections, crystal, square section, crystal, square section, crystal, and eight square sections. (Going backward is the same count, starting with five. It will arrange so that the crystals are scattered.)

Clasp

18. Add two seed beads, go through the clasp ring on the end, add two more seed beads, and go into the bead-work. Go through the work a few times to reinforce the join. Follow the thread path down the side of the bracelet and repeat with the remaining clasp rings.

19. Move through the beadwork to the opposite end of the bracelet. Add the other part of the clasp in the same way. Finish with a half-hitch knot (see page 141), apply bead glue, and cut the thread once dry.

gatsby

THIS BRACELET WEAVES IN AND OUT giving it lots of texture. It's quick to make and is loaded with Czech fire-polished crystals, making it decadent and right out of F. Scott Fitzgerald's *The Great Gatsby*.

The bracelet is mainly made using ladder stitch. What I also like is that even the clasp is made with beads.

Bracelet will be approximately 1″ wide and 7 ¼″ long.

MATERIALS LIST:

.006 Fireline thread

6mm bugle beads, hematite (Fusion Beads, SB0735): 10 grams

8/0 round seed beads, charcoal luster (Fusion Beads, SB1310): 10 grams

11/0 Toho round seed beads, color-lined fuchsia/crystal (Artbeads, TBRD11-350): 8 grams

3mm fire-polished (FP) beads, jet aurora borealis (AB) (Artbeads, FPS-JETAB3): 100

STEPS

1. Cut the thread 1 yard long and thread a needle, leaving a 6" tail.

2. Add two bugle beads and go back through the first one added and again through the second bead. This is ladder stitch. Add another bugle and go through the bead you just exited and again through the one before it.

3. Thread four 8/0 seed beads and attach them to the last bugle you stitched. Go through the four seed beads again.

4. Using ladder stitch (see step 2), add another three bugles. Continue with this pattern of three bugles and one row of seed beads until the bracelet is 1" shorter than the desired length, allowing for the clasp. End with three bugles.

5. Turning back in the opposite direction from where you ended, add nine 11/0 seed beads. Cross over the bugles and meet the opposite end of the closest seed bead row. Go through the seed beads. Repeat to the end of the bracelet.

Frilly Edge

6. Add two 11/0 seed beads, one 3mm FP crystal, and one bead. Go through the FP crystal in the opposite direction. Add two seed beads and go through the next bugle in the ladder. (You may want to tug on your thread and beads a little to snug them up.) Repeat this step on the other side of the bugle and work your way down the ladder to the end of the bracelet.

7. At the end of the ladder, add twelve 11/0 seed beads to form the catch of your clasp. Go through the bugle a few times to reinforce the join.

8. Go through the first bugle and add the same fringe to the bugles on the end for consistency. Go through the beadwork to the other end of the bracelet and do the same.

Toggle Clasp

9. Make a strip of five bugles using ladder stitch (see step 2). Embellish with beads and crystals for frilly edges, like in the bracelet strip (see step 6).

10. Go through the first bugle and the last bugle in the strip to join. Go around the seed beads and FP crystals. Stitch the bugles together.

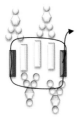

11. Odd-count peyote stitch a strip for the toggle clasp, nine beads long and two wide. This will make a strong chain for your toggle.

   a. Thread eight 11/0 seed beads. Add one 11/0 bead and turn.

   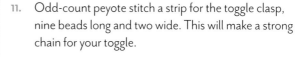

   b. Go through the next bead. Add one bead. Go through the next bead. Continue to end.

   c. Connect the toggle clasp to your strip.

12. Add three 11/0 seed beads, the bugle in the toggle, and three 11/0 seed beads. and go through the bugle you exited to reinforce the join.

stardust

STARDUST IS A DUSTY MATERIAL found between the stars. This bracelet reminds me of stars with stardust all around them. If you create it using all white, it can also resemble snowflakes.

This bracelet uses the right angle weave (RAW) technique.

Bracelet will be approximately ½" wide and 6 ¾" long (10 sections), not including the clasp.

MATERIALS LIST:

.006 Fireline thread

6mm Swarovski crystal pearls, powder rose (Fusion Beads, PL5810): 12

11/0 Toho round seed beads, transparent lustered light gray (Artbeads, TBRD11-112): 8 grams

Medium (13.5mm x 7mm) silver-plated lobster clasp (Artbeads, CLASP11-SP)

Bead glue

STEPS

1. Cut the thread 1 yard long and thread a needle, leaving a 6" tail.

2. Thread a pearl and then seven seed beads. Go around the pearl and through it again.

3. Add seven seed beads. Go around the other direction and through the pearl again.

4. Go through the seed bead above where you exited the pearl. (It will bring the seed bead down to create more-uniform beadwork around the pearl.) Add three seed beads and go back through the seed bead you exited and the first bead you added. This is called a picot.

5. Add two seed beads and go through the next seed bead in the round (shown in red) and the first seed bead you added in the previous step.

6. Go through the two seed beads marked red. Add two seed beads and go through the two beads marked red again. Continue making picots around the pearl.

7. On the last picot add one seed bead—not two. Go through the beads shown in red and back up through the one you just added.

8. Add one seed bead, one pearl, and six seed beads. Go around the pearl and through the single seed bead and pearl you just added.

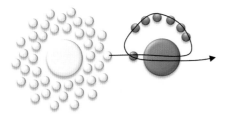

9. Add bottom seed beads around the pearl. Add picots around the beads and continue adding pearls with picots to 6 ¾" long or to the desired length of the bracelet, not including the clasp.

Clasp

10. On one end of the bracelet, add ten seed beads and go back into the beadwork, creating a loop for the lobster clasp. Go through the beads once or twice more to reinforce the loop.

11. Use the tail on the other end of the bracelet, add two seed beads, the lobster clasp, and two seed beads. Go through the work a few times to reinforce the join. Finish with a half-hitch knot (see page 141), apply bead glue, and cut the thread once dry.

crossword puzzle

THE PATTERN ON THIS BRACELET reminds me of the design of a crossword puzzle (if it were covered in gorgeous Swarovski crystals). This bracelet has a lot of texture and two possible styles. By doubling the pattern, you can create a great cuff.

This bracelet uses the right angle weave (RAW) technique.

Single bracelet will be approximately 1 ¼" wide and 6 ¾" long (6 sections), not including the clasp.

Double bracelet will be approximately 2 ½" wide and 6 ¾" long (6 sections), not including the clasp.

MATERIALS LIST:

.008 Fireline thread

8/0 round seed beads, matte black (Fusion Beads, SB1019): 20 grams

1.5mm Toho cube delica beads, metallic amethyst gun metal (Artbeads, TBCB1-90): 8 grams

11/0 Toho round seed beads, moss green-lined yellow (Artbeads, TBRD11-947): 8 grams

4mm Swarovski bicone crystals, peridot aurora borealis (AB) (Artbeads, 5328-PERAB4): 60

30mm x 10mm five-strand tube slide clasp

Bead glue

STEPS

1. Cut the thread 1 yard long and thread a needle, leaving a 6" tail.

2. Add eight 8/0 seed beads and go through the first four again to form a square.

3. Add two 8/0 seed beads and go through the last two beads in the same direction. Go through the two beads you just added. Add six 8/0 seed beads and go through the first two beads you added again. Go through the next four beads you added. Repeat so that you have three squares of beads.

4. Exit from the last two beads added. Add two 8/0 seed beads and again go through the two beads you exited.

5. Add six 8/0 seed beads and go through the two seed beads you added in the previous step and the six new beads.

6. Add two 8/0 seed beads and go back through the last two beads added in the previous step and the two new beads.

7. Add six beads and go through the two beads you added in step 6, completing the square. Continue through the six new beads just added and connect the side squares and the last two you added in this step. Go back around the square. Add a third square in the same way.

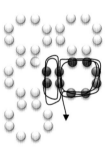

8. Flip your work to match the illustrations for the following steps. Each group of double rows will be separated with two rows of delica beads.

Add two delicas to the side of the top square and go through the two beads you exited at the beginning of the step and the two delicas you just added.

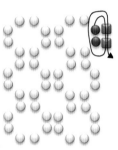

9. Add another set of two delicas to the delicas you just added.

10. Add two 8/0 seed beads to the delicas you just added.

12. Work your way down the width and length to add sections.

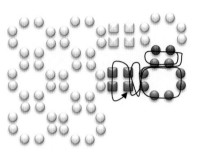

11. Add six 8/0 seed beads to create the first square in the new section.

13. Continue adding sections until your bracelet is the desired length, not including the clasp.

Optional Rows: Add another strip to make an ultrawide cuff. Add cubes between the sections like you did previously. This creates a more uniform look and gives your bracelet a lot of texture.

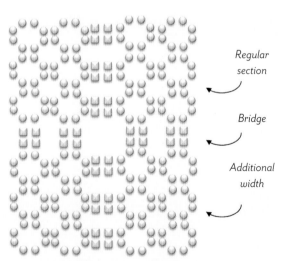

Regular section

Bridge

Additional width

Embellishment

Embellish each of the two-row sections with 11/0 seed beads and bicone crystals.

14. Exit from a corner of a square and add one 11/0 seed bead, one crystal, and one seed bead. Enter on opposite corner to alternate the crystal direction.

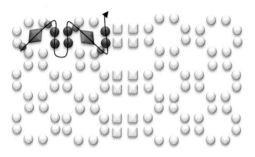

15. Continue to fill in the entire bracelet.

Clasp

16. Add two 11/0 seed beads, go through the clasp ring on the end, add two seed beads, and go into the beadwork. Go through the work a few times to reinforce the join.

    Move through the beadwork to add the next ring of the clasp. Repeat with the remaining rings. Go through the beadwork to the opposite end of the bracelet and attach the remaining part of the clasp. Finish with a half-hitch knot (see page 141), apply bead glue, and cut the thread once dry.

sea gold

MY FAMILY AND I ENJOY WATCHING reality shows where people are tested against the elements. We recently watched a series where people mine the Bering Sea for gold. It was amazing to witness their effort and it was so incredible to see so much gold come up from the floor of the sea. When my daughter saw this bracelet, she said, "It looks just like sea gold!"

The bracelet is made with the peyote stitch.

Bracelet will be approximately ½" wide at its widest point and 7" long, not including the clasp. Each link, when zipped, is ½" wide.

MATERIALS LIST:

.006 Fireline thread

11/0 Miyuki delica beads, trans silver-lined marigold (Artbeads, DB1201): 16 grams

14mm Swarovski cosmic square ring fancy stone crystal frame, bermuda blue (Artbeads, 4437-BRB14): 2

20mm Swarovski cosmic square ring fancy stone crystal frame, bermuda blue (Artbeads, 4437-BRB20): 2

14 mm two-strand box clasp

Bead glue

STEPS

1. Cut the thread 1 yard long and thread a needle, leaving a 6" tail.

2. Take a seed bead that you are not using and thread it. Go through it again to secure it. Do not knot it. You will remove this stop bead by sliding it off when you are ready to add the clasp.

3. Thread four delica beads. Add another delica to make your turn. The first turn can sometimes be tricky. You will want to maintain a consistent tension. Skip the second delica and go through the third delica. Continue this pattern down the row.

4. Thread a delica to make the next turn. Go through the last bead of the row just finished. Continue down the row, filling in each gap the same way you did in the previous step until you have fifteen rows.

5. Make sixteen separate, four-bead-wide strips. Make one strip that is six beads wide (for the center).

6. Form a loop with one of the strips by zippering end to end. To do this, go down through all the beads shown in red.

7. Turn and zip back up from the bottom to the top, going through the beads you skipped in step 6. Finish with a half-hitch knot (see page 141), apply bead glue, and cut the thread once dry.

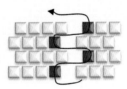

8. Thread another strip inside the first loop you made and zipper up the ends of the strip, linking the loops just like making a paper chain. Continue adding loops until you have six in a row. Before zippering the seventh, add a 14mm crystal frame. Continue adding loops and frames so that the bracelet pattern, end to end, is as follows:

Seven loops, 14mm frame, loop, 20mm frame, six-bead-wide loop, 20mm frame, loop, 14mm frame, seven loops.

Tip: This can get slippery and hard to manage, so put another needle through both sides of the strip while zippering the ends together.

Clasp

9. Remove the stop bead by gently pulling it away from the beadwork. Add two seed beads, one of the clasp rings, and two seed beads. Go back into the beadwork. Go through the work you just did a few times to reinforce the join. Repeat with the other clasp ring. Use the tail to attach the other part of the clasp in the same way. Finish with a half-hitch knot (see page 141), apply bead glue, and cut the thread once dry.

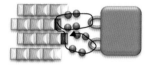

he loves me, he loves me not...

THIS BRACELET REMINDS ME OF A FIELD filled with tiny little flowers. I remember summers as a young girl, running barefoot in the grass, picking flower petals and chanting, "He loves me, he loves me not" and giggling happily when the answer was yes, and even if it was not.

This bracelet uses the triangle technique. Keep your tension consistent but not too tight. It will be difficult to embellish with crystals later if the seed beads are too snug together.

Where you end up after each triangle is important to forming the next triangle properly. How do you end up at the right place? Always go through the beads you just added in every step. Uniform triangles are what you're looking for in this project. Each double set of rows will resemble wagon wheels.

Bracelet will be approximately 1 ¼" wide and 6 ½" long (26 rows), not including the clasp. Add two rows at a time to lengthen. Each set of rows is ½", with nine color A, nine color B, and three bicone crystals.

MATERIALS LIST:

.006 Fireline thread

11/0 Miyuki delica beads, color-lined light amber/amber: 16 grams

3mm fire-polished (FP) crystals, jonquil opal, color A: 117

3mm FP crystals, crystal twilight, color B: 117

3mm Swarovski bicone crystals, Montana sapphire (or pearls): 39

2.5mm x 4.5mm Miyuki Berry Bead, transparent mauve luster: 60

20mm x 10mm three-strand tube slide clasp

Bead glue

STEPS

1. Cut the thread 1 yard long and thread a needle leaving a 6" tail.

2. Thread nine delica beads. Go back through the first six you added.

3. Thread six delicas and go through the last three delicas in the previous step and the six beads you added in this step.

4. Add six delicas. Go through the last three beads in the previous step and the six beads you just added. Repeat step 4 until you have nine triangles.

ROW 2

1. The pattern is as follows: add six delicas, then go through the three before it and the six you just added. Add six delicas, go through the three before and the three just added. Add three delicas and go through the six before and the three just added. Each of the steps in the pattern is shown below. The thread is shown where you should begin the step. As you complete each wagon wheel, you repeat the pattern.

Step 1   Step 2   Step 3

5. Thread six delicas and go through the three previous delicas and the six you just added.

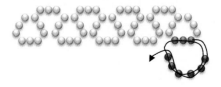

6. Thread six delicas. Go through the beads shown in red.

7. Thread three delicas, creating the last side to the triangle completing the wagon wheel. Go through the beads shown in red and the three you just added.

8. Thread six delicas and go through the three you added in the previous step and the six you just added.

9. Thread three delicas and go through the six shown in red and the three you just added.

ROW 3

1. Starting the third row can be tricky because the ends are not even. If working from left to right, starting from the second triangle in, create your first triangle. Add a triangle to the left of the one you just added and then follow the thread path to the right through the new triangles to continue adding to the row.

Step 1   Step 2   Step 3

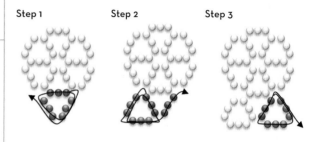

10. Continue adding rows until you reach the desired length of the bracelet, allowing for the clasp.

Embellishment

In order to get the correct pattern, your FP crystals must be lined up in each triangle following the same rule: one end facing the point of the triangle and one end facing the center of the individual triangle, as shown here.

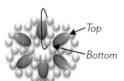

Top

Bottom

11. Following the pattern below, alternate your colors between A and B every three FP crystals (A, A, A, B, B, B, A, A, A). For the second row you will use the opposite pattern (B, B, B, A, A, A, B, B, B).

12. Continue with the pattern shown to embellish the triangles with FP crystals.

13. Go back through the bracelet and add the centers to the flowers using bicone crystals.

14. Follow the thread path to the end of the bracelet. Come out from the corner where there is a natural gap between triangle sections. Add one Berry Bead.

15. Go into the beadwork to the next gap. Add another Berry Bead. Add a Berry Bead to each gap all the way to the corner. (Berry Beads are added to each end before the clasp.)

16. Go through the next three delicas and turn. Add one Berry Bead and go through the last Berry Bead you added.

17. The next four gaps are larger—add two Berry Beads at each gap.

18. On the corner, make the turn and add two Berry Beads. Go through the last two Berry Beads.

19. Add one Berry Bead and then go down through the next two Berry Beads in the previous row. Repeat across to the corner. Go through the last Berry Bead and back into the beadwork so that you can add your clasp.

Clasp

20. Add two delicas, go through the ring on the end of the clasp, add two delicas, and go into the beadwork. Go through the work a few times to reinforce the join. Repeat to attach the remaining clasp rings. Use the tail on the opposite end of the bracelet to add the other part of the clasp. Finish with a half-hitch knot (see page 141), apply bead glue, and cut the thread once dry.

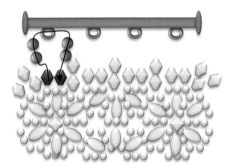

freya

FREYA IS A GODDESS IN NORSE MYTHOLOGY whose most treasured possession, a Brísingamen, was a fantastic and valuable piece of jewelry. Many stories abound on what type it was—many say it was a necklace. I think it was this bracelet.

This bracelet uses a two-drop peyote technique, the right angle weave (RAW) technique, and a bit of wrestling with memory wire.

Bracelet will be approximately ¼" wide and 7 ¼" long (there is no clasp, no overlap). To lengthen, start with longer memory wire.

MATERIALS LIST:

.006 Fireline thread

3mm pearls: 200*

15/0 Toho round seed beads, coordinating color: 3 grams

3mm Swarovski bicone crystals: 9

Memory wire silver-plated oval bracelet .35oz (Artbeads, MWIRE-B3S): 7"

Strong wire cutters (or memory wire cutters)

9mm Swarovski (5500) center-drilled teardrop crystals: 2

Bead glue

* Each section of three pearls is ¼" long. It contains nine additional pearls and several additional seed beads.

STEPS

1. Cut the thread 1 yard long and thread a needle, leaving a 6" tail.

2. String one pearl and two seed beads twenty-five times.

ROWS

3. Add one pearl, bypass the last two seed beads, and go through the last pearl in the previous row.

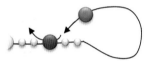

4. Continue down the strip, adding one pearl, bypassing the two seed beads, and going through the next pearl.

5. Make the next turn by adding two seed beads and going down through the last pearl in the previous row.

6. Continue adding two seed beads and passing through the next pearl in the row.

7. Once at the end of the row, make the turn with two seed beads. Go along the row, adding two seed beads and going through the two seed beads from the previous row.

8. Continue along the row until you get to the end. Add one pearl and make your turn. Continue down the row, adding a pearl and passing through two seed beads in the previous row.

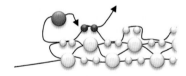

9. Continue until you have six rows of pearls and seed beads.

10. Zip up the two sides of the strip of pearls and seed beads to form a tube. Exit the last two seed beads and cross to the opposite side. Sew through the pearl, cross over to the opposite side of the tube, and sew through that pearl. Continue down the strip.

Tip: Once across, I usually go back down through to the other side to make a strong connection. Continue going up and down to reinforce the tube and leave no gap.

Tube Ends

11. At one end, come up through a pearl and add two seed beads. Go down through the next bead and follow the thread path marked in the illustration. Each time you come up, you will add two seed beads until you complete the circle.

12. For the second round, add two bicone crystals and follow the thread path marked in the illustration to finish the round.

13. For the final round, add one bicone every time you go in and out a bicone in the previous round.

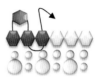

Wire

14. Cut two pieces of memory wire to same length. It should be slightly longer than your pearl tube. Slowly insert memory wire through the tube of beads. Add the second piece of wire.

Tip: You'll need to bend the beadwork because the memory wire will want to come through the side of the tube. You can make the bracelet with one piece of memory wire, but two makes it sturdier.

15. Add a drop of bead glue to ONE wire end and add a teardrop crystal. Push the teardrop until the wire is almost coming through the teardrop, but do not let it come all the way through. You will never be able to get close enough to trim it off once it dries. Let the glue dry. Add a drop of glue to the other end of the wire and glue the other teardrop to it in the same way.

aegis of athena

ATHENA IS THE GODDESS OF WISDOM, courage, civilization, mathematics, strength, strategy, and the arts. She used the Aegis, her shield, for protection. A super hero I grew up admiring wore two large bracelets that were believed to be created from the Aegis of Athena. This bracelet reminds me of them and the added sparkle from the Swarovski crystals between the strips of Herringbone really make it pop. I dare you to wear this and not cross your arms in front of you ready to blast away anything any villain, kid, or husband, throws your way. After all, they're indestructible.

This bracelet uses the herringbone technique (also referred to as ndebele). The added sparkle from the Swarovski crystals between the strips of herringbone really makes it pop. Using large hex beads means this bracelet whips up quickly.

Bracelet will be approximately 2" wide and 7" long, not including the clasp.

MATERIALS LIST:

.006 Fireline thread, crystal

8/0 Toho hex beads, transparent crystal aurora borealis (AB), color A: 8 grams

11/0 delica beads, transparent luster rose gold: 5 grams

8/0 Toho hex beads, matte raku olive/purple, color B: 8 grams

4mm Swarovski bicone crystals, astral pink (5328 Xilion): 53

30mm x 10mm five-strand tube slide clasp

Bead glue

STEPS

1. Cut the thread 1 yard long and thread a needle, leaving a 6" tail.

Center Strip

2. To make a ladder, thread two color A hex beads. Go through both beads again in the same direction. The beads should be side by side with both openings facing up and the closed sides against each other. Add another hex bead and secure it to the bead you just exited. Add more hexes, one at a time, until you have six across.

3. If necessary, flip your work so that your thread is pointing up from the beadwork. Add two color A hexes and go down through the next bead. Come up through the next bead. Add two color A hexes and go down through the next bead. Continue to the end.

4. To turn, add one delica and go up through the last hex added. The delicas will not be on every row; they alternate.

5. Add two color A hexes and go down through the bead in the previous row. (Only go through one row at a time—not all the way to the bottom.) Continue adding beads across to the end. Add one delica to make your turn, as in step 4. Repeat until you have created a bracelet that is 7" long or the desired length, not including the clasp.

6. After stitching the final row, go through each of the beads in the final row, cinching them up to each other to create an identical ladder row to the beginning row. Set aside your work.

Side Strips

7. Make two more strips, using the color B hexes, each one four beads wide and the same length as the one you just created. Do not complete step 6 on the two side strips in order to allow easy addition or removal of beads if they do not line up exactly with the center strip. It can be deceiving when you line them up before joining. Sometimes it looks like they are the same length, but they are actually off by a row or two.

Joining Strips

8. Begin with finished ends and flip the strips so that the outside turn delicas are adjacent and on the same row. Join the delicas together, starting with the first turn delica. Go through the opposite turn delica and add one crystal. Go through them again. Go up through the next delica and down through the delica on the other strip and back up again. Add a crystal. Follow this pattern all the way through to the end.

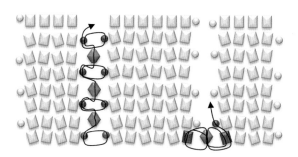

9. After joining the three strips with crystals, go through the beadwork to the end of a side strip. Finish the side strip ends as in step 6.

Clasp

10. Go through the beadwork to one end of the bracelet. Add two delicas, go through the clasp ring on the end, add two delicas, and go into the beadwork. Go through the work a few times to reinforce the join. Secure the remaining rings in the same way. Use the tail on the opposite end of the bracelet and add the other part of the clasp in the same way. Finish with a half-hitch knot (see page 141), apply bead glue, and cut the thread once dry.

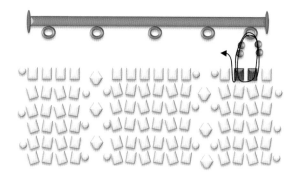

polaris

Polaris is also known as the North Star (and the brightest star). It is located toward the end of the "handle" of the Little Dipper. I must confess: this one is my favorite in the entire book.

This bracelet uses bugle beads, which have sharp ends. Don't pull the thread too tight, or the beads will cut the thread.

Bracelet will be approximately ¾" wide and 6 ½" long (five bugle and seven crystal sections), not including the clasp.

Each section contains eight bugles, eight Swarovski bicone crystals, eight FP crystals, four Superduo beads, and fifty-six seed beads.

MATERIALS LIST:

.006 Fireline thread

Superduo two-hole beads, bronze: 4 grams

4mm Swarovski bicone crystals, astral pink aurora borealis (AB): 40 – 48

12mm twisted bugle beads, matte metallic patina: 40 – 48

11/0 round seed beads, brass-plated metal: 8 grams

3mm Czech fire-polished (FP) crystals: 40 – 48

14mm two-strand gold box clasp

STEPS

1. Cut the thread 1 yard long and thread a needle, leaving a 6" tail.

2. Thread one Superduo, one 4mm crystal, one Superduo, one 4mm crystal, one Superduo, one 4mm crystal, one Superduo, and one 4mm crystal. Go through the beads again to form a circle.

3. Add one 4mm crystal and go through the other/top hole in the Superduo. Add another 4mm crystal and go through the top hole of the next Superduo and continue around in the same way.

4. Pull your thread so that the tension is snug and the crystals are stacked on top of each other.

5. From the top of the Superduo add the following: bugle bead, Superduo, bugle, Superduo, bugle, Superduo, and bugle. Enter the top of the Superduo you exited at the start of this step. Continue all the way around, but instead of going through the top hole of the Superduo you started with, go through the bottom hole of the same Superduo.

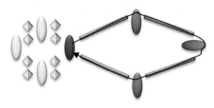

6. Add one bugle and go through the bottom of the next Superduo. Repeat, adding bugles between the existing Superduos, so that you have a stack of two bugles in a diamond shape.

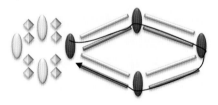

7. Repeat steps 2 to 6 for 6 ½" or the desired bracelet length, not including the clasp. Make sure that you end with a crystal section.

8. Go through the beadwork to the top of a Superduo. Add seven seed beads. Go through the top of the next Superduo, add seven seed beads, and continue around the bugles section.

9. Starting from the Superduo you just exited, pass through five seed beads. Add one FP crystal. Skip two seed beads, one Superduo, and two seed beads and enter the third seed bead. Go through the next two seed beads. Add another FP crystal. Continue around the bugles following the same pattern.

10. Pull your thread so that the FP crystals pull the seed beads. You can go through the crystals and seed beads one more time to make the work secure. Repeat this step for every diamond across the length of the bracelet.

11. Flip your work and repeat steps 8 through 10.

Clasp

12. Go through the beadwork to one end of the bracelet. Add two seed beads, one of the clasp rings, and two seed beads. Go back into the beadwork. Go through the work you just did a few times to reinforce the join. Attach the second ring of the clasp in the same way. Follow the thread path to the opposite end of the bracelet and attach the other part of the clasp in the same way.

faith

I HAPPENED TO FIND THESE NEW CROSS COMPONENTS online and loved the colors that were available. I also like mixing seed beads of various colors for a more casual and playful look. The bracelet is made with multi-color seed beads (mix four of your favorite colors!) and Swarovski crystals.

Bracelet will be approximately ¼" wide and 6 ½" long, not including the clasp. Each spiral is 2" long.

MATERIALS LIST:

.006 Fireline thread

11/0 Toho round seed beads, mixed colors: 8 grams

4mm Swarovski bicone crystals: 20 – 30

32.5mm x 32.5mm x 19.5mm two-hole enameled curved cross link (Fusion Beads, C-Koop Beads)

Bead glue

9mm x 20mm antique bronze round crystal box clasp (Artbeads, BBA-BC01)

STEPS

1. Cut the thread 1 yard long and thread a needle, leaving a 10" tail.

2. Take a seed bead that you are not using and thread it. Put your needle through the bead again to secure it. Do not knot it. You will remove this stop bead when you are ready to add the clasp. Thread seven seed beads. Go through the first four. This completes your first round.

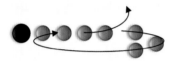

3. Add four seed beads. Go through the last three you added in the previous step and the first new one you added.

4. Add six rounds of seed beads (four seed beads per round). Keep the spiral to one side of your work so that you are consistently adding beads to the correct side and the beadwork gently starts to spiral around the main column of beads. I usually turn the weave and hold each new spiral to the left and add to the right.

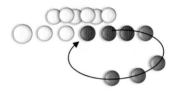

5. On the seventh round, add one seed bead, one crystal, and one seed bead. Go up through the last three seed beads and the first seed bead added in this step.

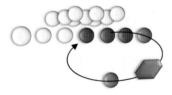

6. Do two rounds of seed beads (repeat step 3) and then repeat step 5. Continue making rounds to create a strand 2 ¼" long. Create another strand just like it.

7. Add four seed beads and the cross pendant. Add four seed beads and go through the seed beads you just added a few times to strengthen the join. Go down into the beadwork and make a half-hitch knot (see page 141), apply bead glue, and trim once dry. Add the remaining strand to the other side of the cross pendant in the same way.

Clasp

8. Remove the stop bead by gently pulling it away from the beadwork. Add three seed beads, the clasp end, and three seed beads. Go back into the beadwork. Go through the work you just did a few times to reinforce the join. Use the tail to the opposite end of the bracelet and attach the other part of the clasp in the same way. Finish with a half-hitch knot (see page 141), apply bead glue, and cut the thread once dry.

brick by brick

THE RULLA BEAD IS PRETTY NEW. I played around with them until I could figure out a pattern. So this design came together brick by brick, and in the end I was happy with it. I hope you will be too.

Bracelet will be approximately 1 ¼" wide and 6 ½" long, not including the clasp.

MATERIALS LIST:

.006 Fireline thread

8/0 hex beads, sparkly rose-lined pale amber (Fusion Beads, SB2694): 10 grams

3mm x 5mm rulla beads, dark bronze (Fusion Beads, SB4394): 20 grams

8/0 Toho round seed beads, dichroic lined cornflower blue rainbow (Artbeads, TBRD8-997): 8 grams

Bead glue

6mm fire-polished (FP) crystals, metallic light blue (Artbeads, FPS-LBL6): 6

19.5mm Swarovski gold-plated filigree daisy, peridot (Artbeads, 62006-GPER): 1

20mm x 9mm round crystal box clasp

STEPS

1. Cut the thread 1 yard long and thread a needle, leaving a 6" tail.

2. Take a seed bead that you are not using and thread it. Put your needle through it again to secure it. Do not knot it. You will remove this stop bead when you are ready to add the clasp. Add one hex, five rullas, and two hexes.

3. Turn your needle to go back through the rulla you just added. You start by flipping the closest rulla so that you can insert your needle through the other hole in the bead.

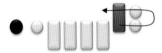

4. Add one rulla. Flip the next rulla and go through the other hole. Add another rulla. Flip the last rulla and go through the other hole. Add two 8/0 seed beads.

5. Add one rulla and go through the next rulla. Add another rulla and pass through the next. Add one more rulla plus two 8/0 seed beads. Go back through the last rulla you added, through the other hole.

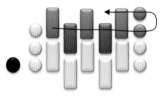

6. Continue adding rows of rullas until you have seven rullas per row. Add one 8/0 seed bead so that your pattern matches the illustration.

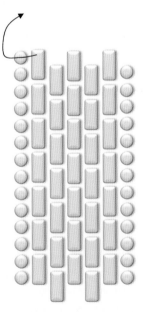

7. Fold the strip in half. At the fold, a few of the beads are now sideways (as shown in dark grey squares). The two ends that are not connected will be different lengths. Flip those beads as shown in the illustration.

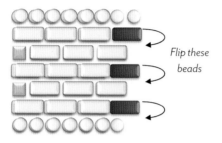

Flip these beads

8. Flip the rullas at the opposite loose end so that you make a clean square. Go through the end of the beads joining the two sides together. When you reach the opposite edge, add one hex. Follow the thread path and go through the seed beads in the strip to reinforce the join.

9. Go through the 8/0 seed beads and two row of rullas on each end of the brick to strengthen and bring them together. Finish with a few half-hitch knots (see page 141), apply bead glue, and cut the thread once dry.

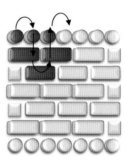

10. Make two medium sections (bricks) of five rullas wide and six rullas long. Make two small bricks of five rullas wide and three rullas long. Make the center focal brick nine rullas wide and nine rullas long.

Attaching Sections

Follow the steps for one side of the bracelet and then repeat for the other side.

11. Select the small block of rullas. Come through the beadwork to exit between the last row of rullas and seed beads. Thread three hexes, one FP crystal, and three hexes, and go into the beadwork on the opposite end of the brick, between the rullas and seed beads. Continue all the way up through the same spot you exited.

12. Select the medium brick of rullas. Go down through the first three hexes you added and the 6mm FP crystal. Add three hexes and enter the next brick through the rullas and seed beads. Continue all the way up through the top of the brick, exiting between the rullas and seed beads. Add three hexes and enter the 6mm FP crystal, continuing through the hexes you just added in this step.

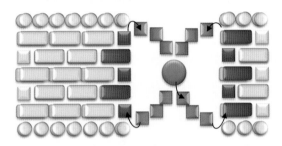

13. Flip the work and repeat the same step adding hex beads but using the existing FP crystal.

14. All the joins will be the same, except when adding the large block in the center since you will add more hex beads to allow for larger brick. Add the sections in this order: small, medium, large, medium, and small. Depending on your clasp, you may need to add more sections.

Center Adornment

15. From the corner of the large brick of rullas, thread four hexes and go through the center of the filigree. Add four more hexes and enter the opposite corner of the rulla brick. Go through the edging of the rulla brick to the nearest corner. Again add four hexes, go through the filigree at the center of the bracelet, add four hexes, and go through the remaining corner. Finish with a half-hitch knot (see page 141), apply bead glue, and cut the thread once dry.

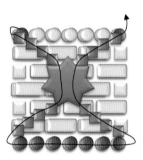

Clasp

16. Remove the stop bead by gently pulling it away from the beadwork. Add three seed beads, the clasp end, and three seed beads. Go back into the beadwork. Go through the work you just did a few times to reinforce the join. Use tail on opposite end of the bracelet and attach the other part of the clasp in the same way. Finish with a half-hitch knot (see page 141), apply bead glue, and cut the thread once dry.

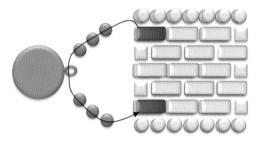

serpentine

THE IDEA CAME TO ME when I saw a woven basket and liked the texture and shades of color as the strips wove in and out. I created this bracelet with that in mind, but I wanted to change both the color and the style of stitch so that it would be obvious that the strip was woven through the beadwork.

This bracelet uses the right angle weave (RAW) technique and the brick stitch.

Bracelet will be approximately ½" wide and 7" long, not including the clasp.

MATERIALS LIST:

.006 Fireline thread

11/0 Toho round seed beads, gold-lustered grey (Artbeads, TBRD11-455) color A: 8 grams

11/0 Toho round seed beads, metallic dark iris aurora borealis (AB) (Artbeads, TBRD11-86) color B: 8 grams

14mm two-strand gold box clasp

Bead glue

STEPS

1. Cut the thread 1 yard long and thread a needle, leaving a 6" tail.

2. Thread eight color A seed beads and tie into a square with a square knot (see page 141).

3. Go back through the first six seed beads.

4. Thread six color A seed beads and go through the last two seed beads in the previous square. Continue through the next four seed beads. Repeat this step one time.

5. On the last square, continue through the next six seed beads (instead of four) so you end up at the bottom of the circle. Thread six color A seed beads and go through the last two seed beads before you exited and the first two you added.

6. Add a second row of squares.

7. Begin the third row of squares. Continue adding squares below this square to form a single column (strip) for thirty-four squares.

8. Add a square to the side of the thirty-four square.

9. Add another square to the side and then complete the base to have two squares by three.

10. Continue adding squares to the third strip to join the opposite base, leaving the center strip open. After the fifth square, join the third strip to the first strip. Go around to the side of the square (shown in red), add two color A seed beads, go through the two beads at the side of the square on the first strip, add two color A seed beads, and join the square you started with by going around the complete path again. Continue adding squares to the third strip. Connect the two strips, leaving a gap of two squares each time.

11. Move to the middle and create the center strip (bridge). Add two color B beads and go through the previous two seed beads and seed beads you just added. This is a brick stitch. Repeat using color B beads so the strip is long enough to weave in and out of the gaps you created in the earlier steps and reach the other end.

12. After weaving the middle strip, attach it to the other end of the bracelet by going through the two seed beads shown in red. Go through the seed beads a few times to reinforce the join.

13. Go through the beadwork to the center bridge over the woven strip. Exit the corner seed bead (a) and add three A seed beads. Enter beadwork at point (b) go through beadwork exiting at point (c), go through the center bead of the three you just added, add another A seed bead, and enter at point (d).

14. Cover the other bridges with the same netting technique.

Clasp

15. Go through the beadwork to one end of the bracelet. Add two color A seed beads, one ring of the clasp end, and two color A seed beads. Go back into the beadwork. Go through the work you just did a few times to reinforce the clasp. Join the other ring of the clasp the same way. Follow the thread path through the beadwork to the opposite end of the bracelet and attach the other part of the clasp in the same way. Finish with a half-hitch knot (see page 141), apply bead glue, and cut the thread once dry.

fleur de lis

MY MOTHER IS FRENCH CANADIAN, and I spent the better part of my youth with my family in Quebec City. The fleur de lis (flower of the lily) appears everywhere as a symbol of their French cultural identity. My fondest childhood memories are from times spent in Quebec. This bracelet uses new beads, lentils, and Rizos to create something that resembles the fleur de lis.

Bracelet will be approximately ¼" wide and 6 ½" long, not including the clasp.

MATERIALS LIST:

.006 Fireline thread

6mm two-hole lentil beads, chartreuse: strand of 50

2.5mm x 6mm Rizo beads, peridot/apollo: 10 grams

11/0 Toho round seed beads, gold-lustered orion: 1 gram

17.5mm clasp with stones (Elegant Elements, Bello Modo CLSP92GP)

Bead glue

STEPS

1. Cut the thread 1 yard long and thread a needle, leaving a 6" tail.

2. Go through a hole in a lentil bead and add three Rizos. Go through the other hole in the lentil.

3. Add a lentil and three Rizos. Come up through the other hole in the lentil. The key to this bracelet is tension, so after you add every lentil/Rizo combo, snug the beads together. To do this, pull the center Rizo of the last three you added with one hand and pull on the lentil with the other.

4. Continue repeating steps 2 and 3 until you reach the desired length of the bracelet, not including the clasp.

Clasp

5. Add three seed beads, the clasp end, and two seed beads. Go back through the last lentil. Go through all of the beads worked in this step a few times to reinforce the join. Follow the thread path to the opposite end of the bracelet and attach the other part of the clasp in the same way. Finish with a half-hitch knot (see page 141), apply bead glue, and cut the thread once dry.

eva

EVERY SPRING AND SUMMER, the flowers come back and so do the colorful and energetic butterflies. I love to see their acrobatics as they bounce from flower to flower, glide through the air, and then flutter back down to another flower with perfect grace. No matter how hard the winter (I told you earlier—I don't like winter), these beautiful creatures return to dance in my garden full of color and life. The smaller crystal sections on this bracelet remind me of butterflies gliding toward the larger, central flower. The name Eva means "Life." This bracelet is for my sister-in-law Eva—who lived life to the fullest.

This bracelet uses a modified right angle weave (RAW) technique.

Bracelet will be approximately ½" wide and 6 ½" long, not including the clasp.

MATERIALS LIST:

.006 Fireline thread

11/0 Toho round seed beads, transparent lustered crystal: 1 gram

20mm x 9mm silver-plated round crystal box clasp (Artbeads, SP-BC01)

4mm Swarovski crystals, Crystal Moonlight: 50

6mm Swarovski pearls, white: 13

6mm Swarovski crystals, Crystal Moonlight: 10

Bead glue

STEPS

1. Cut the thread 1 yard long and thread a needle, leaving a 6" tail.

2. Add ten seed beads. Add your clasp and then go through the beads in the same direction to form a loop for one side of your clasp.

3. Add one seed bead, two 4mm crystals, one seed bead, and one 4mm crystal.

4. Go through the first crystal you added, in the same direction.

5. Add one 4mm crystal, one seed bead, and one 4mm crystal. Go through the crystal you exited at the end of the previous step, in the same direction.

6. Add one seed bead and one 6mm pearl. Repeat steps 3 through 6 four times.

7. Repeat steps 3 through 5 one time using 6mm crystals instead of 4mm crystals. Continue around the cluster.

8. Add a 4mm crystal and go a second time around the beadwork, exiting at the 4mm crystal you just added.

9. Add one 6mm pearl, one 4mm crystal, one 6mm pearl, one 4mm crystal, and one 6mm pearl. Go through the 4mm crystal you exited at the beginning of the step. Continue through the first 4mm crystal you added.

10. Add one 4mm crystal, one seed bead, and one 4mm crystal and go through the 4mm crystal you exited at the beginning of the step.

11. Continue through the first 4mm crystal you added. Add one seed bead and two 4mm crystals and go through the 4mm crystal you exited at the beginning of the step. Continue around the new beads added and then follow the thread path through the pearl and lower 4mm crystal to begin the bottom section.

12. Coming through the bottom 4mm crystal, add one 4mm crystal, one seed bead, and one 4mm crystal. Go through the 4mm crystal you exited at the beginning of this step. Continue through the beads you just added.

13. Add two 4mm crystals and one seed bead. Go through the crystal you exited in the beginning of the step and one more time around the beads you just added. Go through the crystal you exited at the beginning once more and continue through the pearl and the crystal in the top section shown in red.

14. Add a 6mm pearl, one 4mm crystal, and one 6mm pearl. Go into the crystal that you exited at the beginning of this step. Follow the thread path and come through the 4mm crystal you just added.

15. Add one 6mm crystal, one seed bead, and two 6mm crystals and pass through the new beads again.

16. Add one 6mm crystal, one seed bead, and one 6mm crystal. Go through the new beads you added in the same direction, through the 6mm crystal you first exited, and around the three top beads (shown in red).

17. Add one seed bead and one 6mm pearl. Repeat step 4. Continue with steps 4 and 5 until you have four sets of crystals and pearls ending with a pearl.

18. Go through the center 4mm crystal, add three seed beads, and cross over to the outside edge of the crystal shown in red. Go back down through the center crystal, add three seed beads, and go through the crystal shown in green. Flip your work and repeat the same thing on the other side.

19. Continue embellishing ONLY the clusters that have 4mm crystals all the way across the bracelet.

20. Add three seed beads, the clasp end, and three seed beads. Go back into the beadwork. Go through the work you just did a few times to reinforce the clasp. Finish with a half-hitch knot (see page 141), apply bead glue, and cut the thread once dry.

basic techniques

STARTING THE BEADWORK

All of the bracelet instructions begin with a suggested length to cut the thread. In most cases, this amount will be sufficient to complete the entire bracelet. But thread being, well, thread, you might not be comfortable working with the length I suggest. Cut the thread to whatever length you can handle. You can always add more. (See Adding New Thread.)

Weaving is rarely done on two strands. All projects in this book are done on one strand. So start by threading the needle—but don't double it. At the beginning, leave a 6" length of thread (the tail) unworked. Wait to trim your knots until they've been glued and dry. I like to leave my strands long so I know where the knots are—believe it or not, they can disappear into the beadwork easily.

Now follow the instructions for your specific bracelet. You may need to add new thread (see Adding New Thread), add a clasp (see Clasp Notes), or knot the thread (see Knots So Tough).

ADDING NEW THREAD

The best way to add new thread is by tying onto existing woven thread somewhere inside the existing beadwork. You don't just tie the new thread to the old thread (end to end) because it won't fit through the needle and it's not as secure. When the knot is in an interior area of the beadwork (versus the edge), it's less likely to see it when the bracelet is finished.

1. Stop weaving when you have 6" left of your existing thread. With your new thread and leaving another long tail, make a half-hitch knot (see page 141) on the existing thread several beads back from your end point.

2. Weave forward to the point where you left off with the old thread. Tie off the original thread to the work.

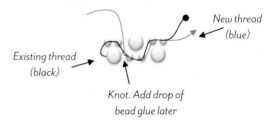

Existing thread (black)

New thread (blue)

Knot. Add drop of bead glue later

3. Weave the new thread into the piece (like it's piggy backing on the old thread) to get to where you will begin beading again. This will strengthen the join.

CLASP NOTES

I like to attach my clasps in the closed position. When you attach the second part to the other end of the bracelet, you'll be abolutely sure that both sides are facing up. It seems obvious, but it's easy to make a mistake. Once you start to attach it, then you can open the clasp to make it easier to work with. Trust me—I've had to remove many a clasp when I've assumed I had it right!

With a multistrand clasp, it's not always possible to line up the beads exactly. Do the best you can with being balanced and centered.

KNOTS SO TOUGH

Whatever knots you make, drop some glue on the knots to make them super secure, and, once dry, trim your threads. I like to use G-S Hypo Cement because it has a really great little applicator that lets me target the knots precisely. Bead glue is very strong and won't ruin your beadwork. Just make sure you wait to let it dry before trimming your work.

Half-Hitch Knot

A half-hitch knot is when you tie a thread onto an existing thread. This knot is used often as a method of tying off your work and adding on thread.

Square Knot

A square knot is simply two overhand knots. It is a good way to create a beaded ring and keep it in place. If you can tie your shoes, you can tie this knot.

THREAD, BEAD, AND NEEDLE CHART

This chart will give you an idea of what thread to use with which size needle and bead.

Beadalon® Wildfire

BEAD SIZE	THREAD SIZE, STRENGTH	NEEDLE SIZE
11/0	.006, 10lb test	10, 12
Larger than 11/0	.008, 12lb test	10

BeadSmith Fireline

BEAD SIZE	THREAD SIZE	NEEDLE SIZE
15/0 to 12/0	.006, 4lb test	12 (and up)
11/0 to 9/0	.008, 6lb test	10
8/0 or larger	.009, 8lb test	10

Nymo Waxed & Unwaxed

BEAD SIZE	THREAD SIZE	NEEDLE SIZE
8/0 or larger	F	10
10/0	D	10
11/0, delica	B	12
13/0 & 14/0	O	13
15/0	OO	16

Resources

ARTBEADS.COM artbeads.com 1-866-715-2323

BEADIN' PATH beadinpath.com 207-650-1557

BELLO MODO bellomodo.com 360-357-3443

FUSION BEADS fusionbeads.com 888-781-3559

MICHAELS STORES, INC. Michaels.com 1-800-642-4235

Acknowledgments

For the amazing friends who helped me with this book, listing you here doesn't feel like it's enough. I truly valued your gracious help. I promise I'll buy lunch: Brette Sember, Heidi Antman, Pernille Jensen, Melissa Monaghan, Melissa Monaghan, and especially Melissa Monaghan.

For my children, Luc, Max, and Annabelle, who never complained when I said, "I can't right now—I have to finish my book." Who always say they like the bracelets when I shove them in their faces and ask, "How's this one?" And who never told Dad when they found beading needles in the bed comforter. (Shhh . . . remember, it's our secret, Annabelle.)

Luc, thank you for controlling your eye rolls when I asked you to check the mail because I was waiting on a bead order.

Annabelle, I'm honestly relieved that I've published before you and look forward to placing your books on my shelf someday.

Max, you cheered for me every day, told everyone you knew about my book, and helped me with ideas. Your enthusiasm was incredible.

And to my husband, David, thank you for running bead kits to my bracelet minions in any weather, picking up finished pieces, and never complaining about it. You're a good husband. You've always let me do whatever the hell I want (and why not?) ;)

My obsession began the first time I took out a bead-weaving book from the North Shore Public Library. Special thanks to them and to the Suffolk County libraries that have hired me over the years to teach beading classes to their patrons. I've enjoyed every moment.

To my incredible agent Jean Martha Sagendorph, who believed in me and made me feel like I was better than I was. I've dreamed of being an author since the 7th grade—thank you for making that dream a reality.

Thanks to Susan Van Horn for her outstanding work on the cover and book design. Your care for your craft shows through, and I certainly appreciate it.

Thanks to the amazing photography by Steve Lagato. Remember—take your family to Quebec City.

Thanks to my smart editor Sophia Muthuraj for patiently guiding me through the process and treating me so well. Thanks also to my technical editor Susan Huxley for being so meticulous and gracious to help make this the best book possible and to the entire team at Running Press.

Index

notes